THE MEANING OF WORK

A Practical Theology of
Work and Rest

Donald McGilchrist

---

with
JIM PETERSEN
TOM PETERSEN
JERRY WHITE

FOURTH EDITION

The Meaning of Work: A Practical Theology of Work and Rest
Copyright © 2021 by Global Commerce Network

All rights reserved. No part of this publication shall be reproduced, stored in a retrieval system, or transmitted by any means, electronic, mechanical, photocopying, recording, or otherwise, without written permission from the publisher.

Global Commerce Network
P.O. Box 51455
Colorado Springs, CO 80949-1455
www.globalcommercenetwork.com

International Standard Book Number (ISBN): 978-1-7358487-6-1

Global Commerce Network is copyrighted and/or registered as a trademark in the United States Patent and Trademark Office by the Global Commerce Network, P.O. Box 51455, Colorado Springs, Colorado 80949-1455.

First Edition February 2003. Third Edition published in 2015. This edition 2021.

The quotations from sources other than the Scriptures have been chosen to amplify or stimulate further thought. They are not necessarily consistent with a biblical worldview.

Scripture taken from the HOLY BIBLE: NEW INTERNATIONAL VERSION®. NIV®. Copyright© 1973, 1978, 1984, 2011 by Biblica, Inc. Used by permission. All rights reserved.

Printed in the United States of America

Contents

Foreword	*5*
Getting the Most Out of This Study	*7*
The Importance of Your Worldview	*9*
What Is the Bible?	*11*
Introduction	*17*
Section 1: The Purpose and Nature of Work	*19*
Section 2: The Great Tragedy	*43*
Section 3: Restoring Work and the Worker	*59*
Section 4: Work as Service	*87*
Section 5: Rest and Recreation	*107*
Taking Action	*141*
Bibliography of Works Cited	*143*

Foreword

Even in Christian circles, many people assume that the Scriptures have little to say about business, innovation, or daily work. This assumption, unfortunately, is based on a long history of misguided thinking that has divided our lives into "secular" and "sacred" compartments. This fragmentation has its consequences. Separating theology from the workplace has frustrated many working men and women, leaving them to feel that their professional lives have no significance in relation to God's purposes in the world.

Having experienced this frustration firsthand, a group of theologians and businessmen set out in the mid-1990s to research what the Scriptures teach about work and commerce. Over the course of six years, they discovered what author Paul Minear stated so well: "The Bible is a book by workers, about workers, for workers." Inspired by what they learned, the original team published six study guides that cover contemporary elements of work, workplace relationships, and economics. This book is the fourth edition of *The Meaning of Work*.

We often refer to the term *commerce*. In our view, commerce includes the broad scope of all economic activity at every level. This definition involves all professions—medicine, teaching, science, construction, military, mining, law. Commerce covers a vast array of interactions. It is highly relational. It plays a significant role in forming the culture in which we live. In fact, very little happens in life without commerce.

God gives us the freedom and responsibility to shape our world (for better or worse). So, as we engage in commerce, our decisions and actions matter not just for our own lives, but also for our communities and even the next generation. This sobering responsibility should compel us to rethink the status quo and to pay close attention to what God desires for work and commerce. After all, he reveals his designs for life not to constrain us but to help us thrive. The Scriptures reveal a God who cares about commerce because he cares about people.

This book and the others in the collection provide a practical and accessible framework to help you explore work and commerce through the lens of the Scriptures. The books will not give you canned answers that force you toward predetermined outcomes, but will help you explore and think about what the Scriptures reveal about your professional life.

Obviously, these books require your time and commitment. We believe this is one of the best attributes of the series! In our hurried and impatient world, we are tempted to skim across an ocean of superficial information, filling our heads with unrelated facts and applying very little of what we learn. Our attention spans wane under an onslaught of unrelated soundbites, tweets, and ads. The cacophony presents us with no purposeful, overarching story. Not surprisingly, we long for meaning. By contrast, these books by GCN Press will help you build your worldview and grow as a person. They encourage us to slow down, think deeply, and live innovatively alongside a committed group of close friends.

Our hope is expressed in our mission statement: "to help men and women align their lives with biblical truth, so that they can survive and flourish in the workplace and spread purpose and hope within their contexts."

Glenn McMahan

Chairman, Global Commerce Network

Getting the Most Out of This Study

This book is designed to help you develop your thinking about one of the most critical matters of human life: your work. It is also designed to be enjoyed in a relational way, for we learn and grow best in iron-sharpens-iron friendships. Engaging with this material together can open the doors to deeper friendships and peer-to-peer business consulting.

Although this study stimulates serious thinking, it is not only an intellectual exercise. What we learn should be lived, and what we live helps us learn. We encourage you to think creatively together about how to apply what you learn from the Scriptures in your workplace and community.

Forming a group is simple. It only takes someone to make the invitations, set a time and place, and create an environment where people feel free to bring questions and insights. The book provides the content and the basic structure for discovery. Facilitators don't need to have all the answers. If you would like to start a group, Global Commerce Network has published a Facilitator's Guide to help.

Many people ask how long it takes to go through the series. That is up to you, but what's the hurry? Some groups study a section at home before meeting together. Others prefer to read and discuss small sections for the first time during each meeting. The important thing is to take your time, think deeply, live what you learn, and enjoy the friendships.

If you need help, write us at: info@globalcommercenetwork.com.

The Importance of Your Worldview

This study, without imposing a dogma, helps us understand and rethink our worldviews in light of the Scriptures. So it might be helpful to understand how our deepest beliefs affect our lives.

Worldview: A worldview is a composite of beliefs, usually adopted from one's culture, media, traditions, family, education, and religion. Every person has a worldview, even if it has been formed in an ad hoc manner. It shapes the way we see and interpret reality, the way we answer the big questions of life: How do we understand the world and its origins? Who are we? What makes life meaningful? What do we believe about God? What happens after death?

Values: Our worldview influences our values. A value is something so important to us that it motivates our actions and decisions. If, for example, we believe there is no life after death, that belief will influence what we find to be most important.

Behavior: In this way, our worldview and values shape our behavior and choices. If self-fulfillment is our primary driving value, our behavior will follow. We will spend a lot of time and energy pursuing things that we hope will satisfy that desire. So our choices and actions each day reflect something about what we really believe.

These three factors serve as a basic framework for understanding ourselves and our society. They also instruct us in how to grow and change. Trying to change just our behavior without addressing our beliefs will usually fail because nothing has changed in our minds!

Worldview is not just a matter of the intellect. The Bible says: "Above all else, guard your heart, for it is the wellspring of life" (Proverbs 4:23). Thus, what you believe about God is influenced by your will and heart. The Scriptures make it clear that if a person's heart is bent on maintaining independence from God, all the best arguments in favor of God won't change anything. The intellect is crucial, but there must also be humility in the heart.

This book presents a theology of work; that is, a view of work that is shaped by a scriptural worldview. It is an opportunity to explore new (and old) ideas, and then to freely reflect on how the Scriptures might reshape your own beliefs, values, and choices.

What Is the Bible?

The Bible is without a doubt the most influential anthology of writings in all of history. Basing their lives on the Bible, men and women have established constitutional governments, opposed totalitarian regimes, ended slavery, developed science, founded universities, worked to cure sickness, served the poor, fought against racism, and humanized commerce. Although it has been terribly misused, the Bible stands as the cornerstone for establishing the infinite and unconditional worth of every human being.

The Bible is a collection of books, a library, written over a period of sixteen hundred years from approximately 1500 BC to 100 AD. Its contents are inextricably rooted in history. The Bible accurately presents specific and testable details about kings, construction, battles, cities, and currencies.

The books of the Bible also portray the full spectrum of human nature. In prose and poetry, the authors express their deepest longings and questions. Others publicly confess their worst behavior and attitudes. King David's adultery, Peter's denial of Christ, Paul's violence against first-century Christians—all the dirt is there for us to read. Clearly, the Bible was not written by public relations specialists trying to put a positive spin on religious ideas. Instead, the Bible is authentic and honest, addressing the complex questions faced by every person.

About forty authors contributed to the Bible. The writers include farmers, soldiers, prophets, kings, musicians, statesmen, fishermen, doctors, and apostles. Given the diversity of the authors and the time span of the writings, one would expect to find an unintelligible hodgepodge of conflicting ideas. To the contrary, there is amazing congruence, with each part contributing to a single, central story. This story is about a just and holy God taking every initiative to show us who he is, what he's like, and how we can live whole and meaningful lives. His motive? He loves us!

The Old Testament provides the history of God's involvement with the nations, primarily with the Israelites. God gradually reveals his holiness, justice, and love. He communicates through the beauty and order of the physical universe, through his messengers (who often wound up murdered), and through his tangible action in history. Many chapters foretell the coming of Jesus, some in great detail. By the time Jesus arrived, most Jewish people knew exactly how to recognize him when they saw him.

The New Testament begins with four accounts of Jesus' life, each from a slightly different perspective. These books are called the Gospels. Then, in the book of Acts, there is a detailed account of the birth of the young churches that sprang up across the Roman Empire in the first century. The remainder of the New Testament consists of personal letters that helped the early faith believers thrive as followers of Christ.

One of those letters, written by Peter, explains why the Scriptures are so extraordinary: "Above all, you must understand that no prophecy of Scripture came about by the prophet's own interpretation. For prophecy never had its origin in the will of man, but men spoke from God as they were carried along by the Holy Spirit."

Because the Bible is thus inspired, it gives us God's wisdom for living a meaningful and joyful life. It addresses issues such as relationships, emotional health, child-rearing, work, business, finances, leadership, and government. As you become familiar with the Bible and benefit from its matchless wisdom, you will understand the importance of Peter's words.

May you be inspired to build, innovate, and serve as you interact with the Bible.

THE MEANING
OF WORK

Introduction

What is usually the most demanding, the most fascinating, and the most frustrating aspect of our lives? Usually it is our work.

Stop and think:

- What does work mean to you and your sense of self-worth?
- What is the "best" kind of work?
- Why is work such a mixture of frustration and challenge?
- What is true rest and how do we balance that with work?

Sampling these questions reminds us that work is an inescapable focus of our lives. Therefore, we must align ourselves with what God wants us to be, do and experience in our work.

We will start with a fresh look at God's original design for our work. Then we will look at the damage done by the Fall, the term often used to describe the results of our rebellion against God. Next we will look at issues such as focus and fulfillment. Is work different from employment? From mere activity? And what is the place for leisure? What type of rest do our souls and bodies need? We will find that living out the kingdom of God in the workplace is radical and countercultural.

What is the connection, then, between our work and God's? What about the pressures of deadlines and the dominance of the bottom line? Through this book, we will equip ourselves to have a meaningful influence in the workplace in ways that are integrated with God's eternal purposes.

SECTION 1
The Purpose and Nature of Work

The Scriptures begin with an account of God at work, creating his universe. We see him organizing, classifying, labeling, blessing, resting. He creates and he develops. He is working with the energy of his Spirit and the wisdom of his Son. This is a willed creation—purposeful, not random, intentional and cumulative, not haphazard.

01 Notice the passion, quality and purposes of God's work in creating the universe. How might this account affect the way you think about your work?

GENESIS 1:1–2:3

In the beginning God created the heavens and the earth. Now the earth was formless and empty, darkness was over the surface of the deep, and the Spirit of God was hovering over the waters.

And God said, "Let there be light," and there was light. God saw that the light was good, and he separated the light from the darkness. God called the light "day," and the darkness he called "night." And there was evening, and there was morning—the first day.

And God said, "Let there be an expanse between the waters to separate water from water." So God made the expanse and separated the water under the expanse from the water above it. And it was so. God called the expanse "sky." And there was evening, and there was morning—the second day.

And God said, "Let the water under the sky be gathered to one place, and let dry ground appear." And it was so. God called the dry ground "land," and the gathered waters he called "seas." And God saw that it was good....

What we see here is a grand entrepreneurial endeavor, purposeful innovation, dedication to functional perfection, commitment to beauty and aesthetics. God's enthusiasm for growth and diversity is contagious. He blesses and takes pleasure in the richness of creation.

. . . Then God said, "Let the land produce vegetation: seed-bearing plants and trees on the land that bear fruit with seed in it, according to their various kinds." And it was so. The land produced vegetation: plants bearing seed according to their kinds and trees bearing fruit with seed in it according to their kinds. And God saw that it was good. And there was evening, and there was morning—the third day.

And God said, "Let there be lights in the expanse of the sky to separate the day from the night, and let them serve as signs to mark seasons and days and years, and let them be lights in the expanse of the sky to give light on the earth." And it was so. God made two great lights—the greater light to govern the day and the lesser light to govern the night. He also made the stars. God set them in the expanse of the sky to give light on the earth, to govern the day and the night, and to separate light from darkness. And God saw that it was good. And there was evening, and there was morning—the fourth day....

God is a worker. This alone tells us that work must be significant, that it must have intrinsic value.

*Doug Sherman &
William Hendricks*

. . . And God said, "Let the water teem with living creatures, and let birds fly above the earth across the expanse of the sky." So God created the great creatures of the sea and every living and moving thing with which the water teems, according to their kinds, and every winged bird according to its kind. And God saw that it was good. God blessed them and said, "Be fruitful and increase in number and fill the water in the seas, and let the birds increase on the earth." And there was evening, and there was morning—the fifth day. . . .

> Adam and Eve . . . cannot treat their environment as an impersonal 'it' because it bears the signature of God and bears his presence and glory. Nor can they worship nature, for that would make nature an idol.
>
> *Paul Stevens*

. . . And God said, "Let the land produce living creatures according to their kinds: livestock, creatures that move along the ground, and wild animals, each according to its kind." And it was so. God made the wild animals according to their kinds, the livestock according to their kinds, and all the creatures that move along the ground according to their kinds. And God saw that it was good. Then God said, "Let us make man in our image, in our likeness, and let them rule over the fish of the sea and the birds of the air, over the livestock, over all the earth, and over all the creatures that move along the ground." . . .

> Repeatedly God describes the capital base he gives us as "good." What do you think that goodness means in this context? Was God's work perfect? Complete? If so, why did he assign responsibilities to us? If not, in what sense is his provision good?

... So God created man in his own image, in the image of God he created him; male and female he created them.

God blessed them and said to them, "Be fruitful and increase in number; fill the earth and subdue it. Rule over the fish of the sea and the birds of the air and over every living creature that moves on the ground."

Then God said, "I give you every seed-bearing plant on the face of the whole earth and every tree that has fruit with seed in it. They will be yours for food. And to all the beasts of the earth and all the birds of the air and all the creatures that move on the ground—everything that has the breath of life in it—I give every green plant for food." And it was so....

Randomness just doesn't cut it when it comes to generating meaningful order out of chaos. Direction is required.... Our universe, tuned so accurately for the needs of intelligent life, indeed ticks to the beat of a very skillful Watchmaker.

Gerald Schroeder, physicist

... God saw all that he had made, and it was very good. And there was evening, and there was morning—the sixth day. Thus the heavens and the earth were completed in all their vast array.

By the seventh day God had finished the work he had been doing; so on the seventh day he rested from all his work. And God blessed the seventh day and made it holy, because on it he rested from all the work of creating that he had done.

Questions

1. Why do you think God embarked on this cosmic entrepreneurial venture? What were God's motivations?

2. Do you think that God needed to rest, or was he setting an example for us? If he was setting an example, why would he be concerned about doing that?

3. Repeatedly, God assesses his work as "good." What do you think this means? Was God's work perfect? Complete?

02 Now we can follow God at work and we can see him sustaining his creation. Consider the range of his activities. What does he do?

PSALM 104:1–24

Praise the LORD, O my soul.

O LORD my God, you are very great; you are clothed with splendor and majesty. He wraps himself in light as with a garment; he stretches out the heavens like a tent and lays the beams of his upper chambers on their waters. He makes the clouds his chariot and rides on the wings of the wind. He makes winds his messengers, flames of fire his servants.

He set the earth on its foundations; it can never be moved. You covered it with the deep as with a garment; the waters stood above the mountains. But at your rebuke the waters fled, at the sound of your thunder they took to flight; they flowed over the mountains, they went down into the valleys, to the place you assigned for them. You set a boundary they cannot cross; never again will they cover the earth.

He makes springs pour water into the ravines; it flows between the mountains. They give water to all the beasts of the field; the wild donkeys quench their thirst. The birds of the air nest by the waters; they sing among the branches. He waters the mountains from his upper chambers; the earth is satisfied by the fruit of his work. He makes grass grow for the cattle, and plants for man to cultivate—bringing forth food from the earth: wine that gladdens the heart of man, oil to make his face shine, and bread that sustains his heart. The trees of the LORD are well watered, the cedars of Lebanon that he planted. There the birds make their nests; the stork has its home in the pine trees. The high mountains belong to the wild goats; the crags are a refuge for the coneys....

... The moon marks off the seasons, and the sun knows when to go down. You bring darkness, it becomes night, and all the beasts of the forest prowl. The lions roar for their prey and seek their food from God. The sun rises, and they steal away; they return and lie down in their dens. Then man goes out to his work, to his labor until evening. How many are your works, O LORD! In wisdom you made them all; the earth is full of your creatures.

Men and women in the Old and New Testaments worked in a wide variety of jobs. These included: apothecary, baker, boat builder, carpenter, druggist, fisherman, goldsmith, historian, king, lawyer, mason, musician, painter, poet, priest, ropemaker, shepherd, toolmaker, weaver, and winemaker.

COLOSSIANS 1:15–20

He [Jesus] is the image of the invisible God, the firstborn over all creation. For by him all things were created: things in heaven and on earth, visible and invisible, whether thrones or powers or rulers or authorities; all things were created by him and for him. He is before all things, and in him all things hold together. And he is the head of the body, the church; he is the beginning and the firstborn from among the dead, so that in everything he might have the supremacy. For God was pleased to have all his fullness dwell in him, and through him to reconcile to himself all things, whether things on earth or things in heaven, by making peace through his blood, shed on the cross.

In the divine economy, work is evaluated according to the way it fosters or retards relationships—between ourselves and God, our companions and the earthly resources we are called to develop.

Gordon Preece

Astronomy leads us to a unique event, a universe that
was created out of nothing, one with the very delicate
balance needed to provide exactly the conditions
required to permit life, and one which has an underlying
(one might say "supernatural") plan.

Nobel Prize winner Arno Penzias

Questions

1. God sustains creation. How does this affect our view of work?

2. Describe the interplay between what God does and what his creatures do in response to him.

3. Based on what you read in Psalm 104, how would you distinguish the role of man from that of other creatures?

03 Drawing from Psalm 111, explore the connections between God's work and his character.

PSALM 111:1–10

I will extol the LORD with all my heart in the council of the upright and in the assembly. Great are the works of the LORD; they are pondered by all who delight in them. Glorious and majestic are his deeds, and his righteousness endures forever. He has caused his wonders to be remembered; the LORD is gracious and compassionate. He provides food for those who fear him; he remembers his covenant forever. He has shown his people the power of his works, giving them the lands of other nations. The works of his hands are faithful and just; all his precepts are trustworthy. They are steadfast for ever and ever, done in faithfulness and uprightness. He provided redemption for his people; he ordained his covenant forever— holy and awesome is his name. The fear of the LORD is the beginning of wisdom; all who follow his precepts have good understanding. To him belongs eternal praise.

> Since work was given before the Fall, it has intrinsic value (it is good in itself and may even be therapeutic), instrumental value (it meets needs and creates edifying results) and spiritual value (it is a way of loving God and being loved by him).
>
> *Paul Stevens*

Questions

1. Summarize how God's actions reveal his nature.
2. How does character influence the way we work?

04 Notice how the Scriptures use metaphors about work to describe God.

PSALM 23:1–6

The LORD is my shepherd, I shall not be in want. He makes me lie down in green pastures, he leads me beside quiet waters, he restores my soul. He guides me in paths of righteousness for his name's sake. Even though I walk through the valley of the shadow of death, I will fear no evil, for you are with me; your rod and your staff, they comfort me.

You prepare a table before me in the

presence of my enemies. You anoint my head with oil; my cup overflows. Surely goodness and love will follow me all the days of my life, and I will dwell in the house of the LORD forever.

ISAIAH 64:8

Yet, O LORD, you are our Father. We are the clay, you are the potter; we are all the work of your hand.

JOHN 15:1–8

I am the true vine, and my Father is the gardener. He cuts off every branch in me that bears no fruit, while every branch that does bear fruit he prunes so that it will be even more fruitful. You are already clean because of the word I have spoken to you. Remain in me, and I will remain in you. No branch can bear fruit by itself; it must remain in the vine. Neither can you bear fruit unless you remain in me.

I am the vine; you are the branches. If a man remains in me and I in him, he will bear much fruit; apart from me you can do nothing. If anyone does not remain in me, he is like a branch that is thrown away and withers; such branches are picked up, thrown into the fire and burned. If you remain in me and my words remain in you, ask whatever you wish, and it will be given you. This is to my Father's glory, that you bear much fruit, showing yourselves to be my disciples.

> The parables of Jesus refer to occupations such as sowing (Matthew 13:30), laboring in a vineyard (Matthew 13:30), harvesting (John 4:35), building a house (Matthew 7:24), caring for pigs (Luke 15:11) . . . thereby lending dignity to human work.

Questions

1. What do these everyday images suggest about God's view of the importance of human occupations?

2. Why do you suppose God uses such common metaphors?

05 God has provided a set of assignments that form a broad "job description" for us. These assignments are mentioned in the following passages. What are our responsibilities?

GENESIS 1:27–30

So God created man in his own image, in the image of God he created him; male and female he created them.

God blessed them and said to them, "Be fruitful and increase in number; fill the earth and subdue it. Rule over the fish of the sea and the birds of the air and over every living creature that moves on the ground."

Then God said, "I give you every seed-bearing plant on the face of the whole earth and every tree that has fruit with seed in it. They will be yours for food. And to all the beasts of the earth and all the birds of the air and all the creatures that move on the ground—everything that has the breath of life in it—I give every green plant for food." And it was so.

In these two scriptures (above and below), we see a call to be productive while also conserving nature. How is this working out today?

GENESIS 2:15

The LORD God took the man and put him in the Garden of Eden to work it and take care of it.

> Man is a maker, who makes things because he wants to, because he cannot fulfill his true nature if he is prevented from making things . . .; he is made in the image of the Maker and he must himself create or become something less than a man.
>
> *Dorothy Sayers*

GENESIS 2:19–20

Now the LORD God had formed out of the ground all the beasts of the field and all the birds of the air. He brought them to the man to see what he would name them; and whatever the man called each living creature, that was its name. So the man gave names to all the livestock, the birds of the air and all the beasts of the field. But for Adam no suitable helper was found.

> By delegating the naming of the creatures to us, God demonstrated the authority that he had placed in our hands. He conveyed ownership to us.

GENESIS 9:1–7

Then God blessed Noah and his sons, saying to them, "Be fruitful and increase in number and fill the earth. The fear and dread of you will fall upon all the beasts of the earth and all the birds of the air, upon every creature that moves along the ground, and upon all the fish of the sea; they are given into your hands. Everything that lives and moves will be food for you. Just as I gave you the green plants, I now give you everything.

But you must not eat meat that has its lifeblood still in it. And for your lifeblood I will surely demand an accounting. I will demand an accounting from every animal. And from each man, too, I will demand an accounting for the life of his fellow man.

Whoever sheds the blood of man, by man shall his blood be shed; for in the image of God has God made man. As for you, be fruitful and increase in number; multiply on the earth and increase upon it.

EPHESIANS 1:11-12 (THE MESSAGE)

It's in Christ that we find out who we are and what we are living for. Long before we first heard of Christ and got our hopes up, he had his eye on us, had designs on us for glorious living, part of the overall purpose he is working out in everything and everyone.

PSALM 115:16

The highest heavens belong to the LORD, but the earth he has given to man.

Questions

1. Summarize the work, which is sometimes called the creational or the cultural mandate, that God intends for us.

2. As for God's work, what distinguishes human beings from the rest of his creation?

06 From the following scriptures, take note of the reasons why God wants us to work.

ECCLESIASTES 3:13

That everyone may eat and drink, and find satisfaction in all his toil— this is the gift of God.

MATTHEW 5:16

In the same way, let your light shine before men, that they may see your good deeds and praise your Father in heaven.

> Every day, millions of workers go to work without seeing the slightest connection between what they do all day and what they think God wants done in the world.
>
> *Doug Sherman & William Hendricks*

ACTS 20:33–35

I have not coveted anyone's silver or gold or clothing. You yourselves know that these hands of mine have supplied my own needs and the needs of my companions. In everything I did, I showed you that by this kind of hard work we must help the weak, remembering the words the Lord Jesus himself said: 'It is more blessed to give than to receive.'

1 CORINTHIANS 10:31

So whether you eat or drink or whatever you do, do it all for the glory of God.

Work is an expenditure of energy in service which brings fulfillment to the worker, benefit to the community, and glory to God.

John Stott

EPHESIANS 4:28

He who has been stealing must steal no longer, but must work, doing something useful with his own hands, that he may have something to share with those in need.

1 THESSALONIANS 4:9–12

Now about brotherly love we do not need to write to you, for you yourselves have been taught by God to love each other. And in fact, you do love all the brothers throughout Macedonia. Yet we urge you, brothers, to do so more and more. Make it your ambition to lead a quiet life, to mind your own business and to work with your hands, just as we told you, so that your daily life may win the respect of outsiders and so that you will not be dependent on anybody.

2 THESSALONIANS 3:6–12

In the name of the Lord Jesus Christ, we command you, brothers, to keep away from every brother who is idle and does not live according to the teaching you received from us. For you yourselves know how you ought to follow our example. We were not idle when we were with you, nor did we eat anyone's food without paying for it. On the contrary, we worked night and day, laboring and toiling so that we would not be a burden to any of you. We did this, not because we do not have the right to such help, but in order to make ourselves a model for you to follow. For even when we were with you, we gave you this rule: "If a man will not work, he shall not eat."

We hear that some among you are idle. They are not busy; they are busybodies. Such people we command and urge in the Lord Jesus Christ to settle down and earn the bread they eat.

> The word "company" is derived from two Latin roots: *com* and *panis*, "together" and "bread." Hence, it meant associates or companions who are close enough to share meals together. The word "corporation" is derived from the Latin root for a body. Thus, it meant persons authorized to act as one body. It reminds us of Paul's metaphor of the Corpus Christi, or Body of Christ.

TITUS 3:14

Our people must learn to devote themselves to doing what is good, in order that they may provide for daily necessities and not live unproductive lives.

1 PETER 2:12

Live such good lives among the pagans that, though they accuse you of doing wrong, they may see your good deeds and glorify God on the day he visits us.

> In what ways do good lives and good deeds glorify God?

Questions

1. Summarize the reasons why God wants us to work.
2. Should I look to God, to my work, or to my family to supply my needs—or should I look to all three sources?

3. We are not designed to be solitary individuals. Summarize how your work plays a role in fulfilling social responsibilities.

4. Compare a biblical definition of work with these secular definitions:
    a. Intentional activity to accomplish a result.
    b. The commitment of energy to supply a product.

5. How do the Scriptures enrich the significance of work?

6. In light of all you have considered, what is work?

07 God is concerned about every detail of our work. What do you observe from the following example?

ISAIAH 28:23–29

Listen and hear my voice; pay attention and hear what I say. When a farmer plows for planting, does he plow continually? Does he keep on breaking up and harrowing the soil? When he has leveled the surface, does he not sow caraway and scatter cummin? Does he not plant wheat in its place, barley in its plot, and spelt in its field? His God instructs him and teaches him the right way. Caraway is not threshed with a sledge, nor is a cartwheel rolled over cummin; caraway is beaten out with a rod, and cummin with a stick. Grain must be ground to make bread; so one does not go on threshing it forever. Though he drives the wheels of his threshing cart over it, his horses do not grind it. All this also comes from the LORD Almighty, wonderful in counsel and magnificent in wisdom.

Sowing (v23–26) and reaping (v27–28) in the scripture above are not only purposeful, but specialized: Work has to be appropriate and discriminating.

Questions

1. How does God's concern for us affect our approach to the intricacies of daily life?

08 How does our work interface with God's work?

Secular work is spiritual if your focus is eternal and spiritual work is secular if your focus is temporal.

NEHEMIAH 4:6–15

So we rebuilt the wall till all of it reached half its height, for the people worked with all their heart. But when Sanballat, Tobiah, the Arabs, the Ammonites and the men of Ashdod heard that the repairs to Jerusalem's walls had gone ahead and that the gaps were being closed, they were very angry. They all plotted together to come and fight against Jerusalem and stir up trouble against it. But we prayed to our God and posted a guard day and night to meet this threat.

Meanwhile, the people in Judah said, "The strength of the laborers is giving out, and there is so much rubble that we cannot rebuild the wall."

Also our enemies said, "Before they know it or see us, we will be right there among them and will kill them and put an end to the work."

Then the Jews who lived near them came and told us ten times over, "Wherever you turn, they will attack us."

Therefore I stationed some of the people behind the lowest points of the wall at the exposed places, posting them by families, with their swords, spears and bows. After I looked things over, I stood up and said to the nobles, the officials and the rest of the people, "Don't be afraid of them. Remember the Lord, who is great and awesome, and fight for your brothers, your sons and your daughters, your wives and your homes."

When our enemies heard that we were aware of their plot and that God had frustrated it, we all returned to the wall, each to his own work.

Observe that the only person of whom the Old Testament declares that he was "filled with the Spirit of God" was Bezalel, a skilled craftsman (Exodus 31:1–5).

NEHEMIAH 6:16

When all our enemies heard about this, all the surrounding nations were afraid and lost their self-confidence, because they realized that this work had been done with the help of our God.

William Tyndale, who was burned at the stake for heresy in 1536, was prosecuted in part because of his biblical view of work, saying: "There is no work better than another to please God; to pour water, to wash dishes, to be a cobbler or an apostle, all is one; to wash dishes and to preach is all one, as touching the deed, to please God."

---

1 CORINTHIANS 3:5–15

What, after all, is Apollos? And what is Paul? Only servants, through whom you came to believe—as the Lord has assigned to each his task. I planted the seed, Apollos watered it, but God made it grow. So neither he who plants nor he who waters is anything, but only God, who makes things grow. The man who plants and the man who waters have one purpose, and each will be rewarded according to his own labor. For we are God's fellow workers; you are God's field, God's building.

By the grace God has given me, I laid a foundation as an expert builder, and someone else is building on it. But each one should be careful how he builds. For no one can lay any foundation other than the one already laid, which is Jesus Christ. If any man builds on this foundation using gold, silver, costly stones, wood, hay or straw, his work will be shown for what it is, because the Day will bring it to light. It will be revealed with fire, and the fire will test the quality of each man's work. If what he has built survives, he will receive his reward. If it is burned up, he will suffer loss; he himself will be saved, but only as one escaping through the flames.

PHILIPPIANS 2:12–13

Therefore, my dear friends, as you have always obeyed—not only in my presence, but now much more in my absence—continue to work out your salvation with fear and trembling, for it is God who works in you to will and to act according to his good purpose.

1 CORINTHIANS 15:10

But by the grace of God I am what I am, and his grace to me is not without effect. No, I worked harder than all of them—yet not I, but the grace of God that was with me.

COLOSSIANS 1:28–29

We proclaim him, admonishing and teaching everyone with all wisdom, so that we may present everyone perfect in Christ. To this end I labor, struggling with all his energy, which so powerfully works in me.

Questions

1. Summarize the dynamics between our responsibility and God's responsibility.

2. "For we are God's workmanship, created in Christ Jesus to do good works, which God prepared in advance for us to do" (Ephesians 2:10). We see here that God is going before us, preparing a way. How does Paul's affirmation help us, as workers, connect with the purposes of God?

Section 1 reveals that work is profoundly important to God and that our work should be an extension of his work. Our conduct in business reveals who we are; it displays our values. Indeed, we should work in such a way that our actions remind people of God.

Many men and women work as if they are independent of God, but we can never escape our dependence on his provision. We should be energetic and creative while looking to God to provide for us.

Why should we work? The overarching reason is that we were made to glorify God (Isaiah 43:7). We were chosen to be for the praise of God's glory (1 Corinthians 10:31). In short, this means that we are to reflect God's nature in all we do. We must neither descend to the instinctive plane of animals nor arrogantly usurp God's prerogatives. He has given us almost unlimited resources and he expects us to use them for his purposes. How does your business reflect God's nature?

Section Notes

SECTION 2
The Great Tragedy

Even in ancient Greek literature, we see the the concept of tragedy. Someone of great worth falls and fails. As a result, he or she lands in terrible circumstances. Thus, for a scenario to be "tragic" there must be a "fall" from original dignity.

That is, essentially, what the Scriptures call "sin." It all started with a willful rebellion against God—a pursuit of our autonomy, an effort to fly solo without God. This separation from God, freely chosen by us, has downstream consequences. It radically alters our relationships and naturally makes work harder. Outside of God's designs for life, work becomes toil.

In this section we will study the tragedy of sin, and in the next section we will consider how Jesus restored a way back to a relationship with God. This brings new dignity, peace, and significance to us as workers.

09 Here is the account of how Adam and Eve broke their relationship with God, an event that is often referred to as "the Fall." What happened? How did God handle it? What issues come to mind as you read these scriptures?

GENESIS 3:1-23

Now the serpent was more crafty than any of the wild animals the LORD God had made. He said to the woman, "Did God really say, 'You must not eat from any tree in the garden'?"

The woman said to the serpent, "We may eat fruit from the trees in the garden, but God did say, 'You must not eat fruit from the tree that is in the middle of the garden, and you must not touch it, or you will die.'"

The slide into sin is evident. There is an appeal to the ego combined with a lie that says there will be no consequences for our turn away from God. Then reality sets in. We are filled with guilt and shame, which causes us to hide from God and one another. This is a death spiral. What saves us?

"You will not surely die," the serpent said to the woman. "For God knows that when you eat of it your eyes will be opened, and you will be like God, knowing good and evil."

When the woman saw that the fruit of the tree was good for food and pleasing to the eye, and also desirable for gaining wisdom, she took some and ate it. She also gave some to her husband, who was with her, and he ate it. Then the eyes of both of them were opened, and they realized they were naked; so they sewed fig leaves together and made coverings for themselves. . . .

> God comes looking for his friends. Sadly, the final recovery of full companionship will have to wait until the New Jerusalem, where "God Himself will be with them and be their God" (Revelation 21:3–4). Meanwhile, our God persistently pursues us.

... Then the man and his wife heard the sound of the LORD God as he was walking in the garden in the cool of the day, and they hid from the LORD God among the trees of the garden. But the LORD God called to the man, "Where are you?"

He answered, "I heard you in the garden, and I was afraid because I was naked; so I hid."

And he said, "Who told you that you were naked? Have you eaten from the tree that I commanded you not to eat from?"

The man said, "The woman you put here with me—she gave me some fruit from the tree, and I ate it."

Then the LORD God said to the woman, "What is this you have done?"

The woman said, "The serpent deceived me, and I ate."

So the LORD God said to the serpent, "Because you have done this, "Cursed are you above all the livestock and all the wild animals! You will crawl on your belly and you will eat dust all the days of your life. And I will put enmity between you and the woman, and between your offspring and hers; he will crush your head, and you will strike his heel...."

> Adam and Eve chose to disobey God by rejecting how they were created, designed, tasked, sustained, and blessed. Their primal sin in the garden separated us from God, from one another, and from all that God had made. All of our relationships were damaged.

... To the woman he said, "I will greatly increase your pains in childbearing; with pain you will give birth to children. Your desire will be for your husband, and he will rule over you."

To Adam he said, "Because you listened to your wife and ate from the tree about which I commanded you, 'You must not eat of it,' cursed is the ground because of you; through painful toil you will eat of it all the days of your life. It will produce thorns and thistles for you, and you will eat the plants of the field. By the sweat of your brow you will eat your food until you return to the ground, since from it you were taken; for dust you are and to dust you will return."

Adam named his wife Eve, because she would become the mother of all the living. ...

This tree of life, from which we are separated, appears again beside the river of life in the New Jerusalem ... with leaves for the healing of the nations. (See Revelation 22:1-4)

... The LORD God made garments of skin for Adam and his wife and clothed them. And the LORD God said, "The man has now become like one of us, knowing good and evil. He must not be allowed to reach out his hand and take also from the tree of life and eat, and live forever." So the LORD God banished him from the Garden of Eden to work the ground from which he had been taken.

The process of God's good creation was thrust into reverse: from light to darkness, from order to chaos, from dignity to degradation. The universe became abnormal. It is now in "bondage to decay" (Romans 8:21).

GENESIS 4:8–26

Now Cain said to his brother Abel, "Let's go out to the field." And while they were in the field, Cain attacked his brother Abel and killed him.

Then the LORD said to Cain, "Where is your brother Abel?"

"I don't know," he replied. "Am I my brother's keeper?"

The LORD said, "What have you done? Listen! Your brother's blood cries out to me from the ground. Now you are under a curse and driven from the ground, which opened its mouth to receive your brother's blood from your hand. When you work the ground, it will no longer yield its crops for you. You will be a restless wanderer on the earth."

Cain said to the LORD, "My punishment is more than I can bear. Today you are driving me from the land, and I will be hidden from your presence; I will be a restless wanderer on the earth, and whoever finds me will kill me."

But the LORD said to him, "Not so; if anyone kills Cain, he will suffer vengeance seven times over." Then the LORD put a mark on Cain so that no one who found him would kill him. So Cain went out from the LORD'S presence and lived in the land of Nod, east of Eden....

Cain's family is a microcosm: Its pattern of technical prowess and moral failure is that of humanity.

Derek Kidner

... Cain lay with his wife, and she became pregnant and gave birth to Enoch. Cain was then building a city, and he named it after his son Enoch. To Enoch was born Irad, and Irad was the father of Mehujael, and Mehujael was the father of Methushael, and Methushael was the father of Lamech.

Lamech married two women, one named Adah and the other Zillah. Adah gave birth to Jabal; he was the father of those who live in tents and raise livestock. His brother's name was Jubal; he was the father of all who play the harp and flute. Zillah also had a son, Tubal-Cain, who forged all kinds of tools out of bronze and iron. Tubal-Cain's sister was Naamah....

Lamech said to his wives, "Adah and Zillah, listen to me; wives of Lamech, hear my words. I have killed a man for wounding me, a young man for injuring me. If Cain is avenged seven times, then Lamech seventy-seven times."

Adam lay with his wife again, and she gave birth to a son and named him Seth, saying, "God has granted me another child in place of Abel, since Cain killed him." Seth also had a son, and he named him Enosh.

At that time men began to call on the name of the LORD.

Purpose belongs to persons, function belongs to things.

Harry Blamires

GENESIS 5:28–29

When Lamech had lived 182 years, he had a son. He named him Noah and said, "He will comfort us in the labor and painful toil of our hands caused by the ground the LORD has cursed."

Questions

1. How has sin altered:
    a. the worker?
    b. the work?
    c. the context in which we work?

10 Sin changes and damages everything. From the following scriptures, record your observations of the damage.

ECCLESIASTES 2:1–11

I thought in my heart, "Come now, I will test you with pleasure to find out what is good." But that also proved to be meaningless. "Laughter," I said, "is foolish. And what does pleasure accomplish?" I tried cheering myself with wine, and embracing folly—my mind still guiding me with wisdom. I wanted to see what was worthwhile for men to do under heaven during the few days of their lives....

Achievement crumbles . . . motivation sags . . . mortality looms.

. . . I undertook great projects: I built houses for myself and planted vineyards. I made gardens and parks and planted all kinds of fruit trees in them. I made reservoirs to water groves of flourishing trees. I bought male and female slaves and had other slaves who were born in my house. I also owned more herds and flocks than anyone in Jerusalem before me. I amassed silver and gold for myself, and the treasure of kings and provinces. I acquired men and women singers, and a harem as well—the delights of the heart of man. I became greater by far than anyone in Jerusalem before me. In all this my wisdom stayed with me....

The intimate bond between producing and consuming is broken.

... I denied myself nothing my eyes desired; I refused my heart no pleasure. My heart took delight in all my work, and this was the reward for all my labor. Yet when I surveyed all that my hands had done and what I had toiled to achieve, everything was meaningless, a chasing after the wind; nothing was gained under the sun.

Jesus himself spoke of the 'new birth' of the world at his coming; Peter of the 'restoration' of all things; Paul here of the liberation, and elsewhere of the reconciliation, of all things; and John of the new heaven and earth, in which God will dwell with His people. . . . The future glory is beyond our imagination. What we do know is that God's material creation will be redeemed and glorified, because God's children will be redeemed and glorified.

John Stott, on Romans 8:20-22

ECCLESIASTES 2:17–23

So I hated life, because the work that is done under the sun was grievous to me. All of it is meaningless, a chasing after the wind. I hated all the things I had toiled for under the sun, because I must leave them to the one who comes after me. And who knows whether he will be a wise man or a fool? Yet he will have control over all the work into which I have poured my effort and skill under the sun. This too is meaningless. So my heart began to despair over all my toilsome labor under the sun. For a man may do his work with wisdom, knowledge and skill, and then he must leave all he owns to someone who has not worked for it. This too is meaningless and a great misfortune. What does a man get for all the toil and anxious striving with which he labors under the sun? All his days his work is pain and grief; even at night his mind does not rest. This too is meaningless.

ROMANS 8:18–22

I consider that our present sufferings are not worth comparing with the glory that will be revealed in us. The creation waits in eager expectation for the sons of God to be revealed. For the creation was subjected to frustration, not by its own choice, but by the will of the one who subjected it, in hope that the creation itself will be liberated from its bondage to decay and brought into the glorious freedom of the children of God. We know that the whole creation has been groaning as in the pains of childbirth right up to the present time.

Questions

1. How has sin damaged the entire creation?

2. How do sin and a sense of futility affect our attitudes about work?

11 Consider the following scriptures and draw out the aspects of human work that displease God.

Only a few are left who think of what they are doing as work, rather than as making a living.

Hannah Arendt

GENESIS 11:1–9

Now the whole world had one language and a common speech. As men moved eastward, they found a plain in Shinar and settled there.

They said to each other, "Come, let's make bricks and bake them thoroughly." They used brick instead of stone, and tar for mortar. Then they said, "Come, let us build ourselves a city, with a tower that reaches to the heavens, so that we may make a name for ourselves and not be scattered over the face of the whole earth."

But the LORD came down to see the city and the tower that the men were building. The LORD said, "If as one people speaking the same language they have begun to do this, then nothing they plan to do will be impossible for them. Come, let us go down and confuse their language so they will not understand each other."

So the LORD scattered them from there over all the earth, and they stopped building the city. That is why it was called Babel—because there the LORD confused the language of the whole world. From there the LORD scattered them over the face of the whole earth.

Work is not the curse, but drudgery is.

Henry Ward Beecher

EXODUS 20:8–11

Remember the Sabbath day by keeping it holy. Six days you shall labor and do all your work, but the seventh day is a Sabbath to the LORD your God. On it you shall not do any work, neither you, nor your son or daughter, nor your manservant or maidservant, nor your animals, nor the alien within your gates. For in six days the LORD made the heavens and the earth, the sea, and all that is in them, but he rested on the seventh day. Therefore the LORD blessed the Sabbath day and made it holy.

PSALM 127:1–2

Unless the LORD builds the house, its builders labor in vain. Unless the LORD watches over the city, the watchmen stand guard in vain. In vain you rise early and stay up late, toiling for food to eat—for he grants sleep to those he loves.

ISAIAH 44:9–20

All who make idols are nothing, and the things they treasure are worthless. Those who would speak up for them are blind; they are ignorant, to their own shame. Who shapes a god and casts an idol, which can profit him nothing? He and his kind will be put to shame; craftsmen are nothing but men. Let them all come together and take their stand; they will be brought down to terror and infamy. . . .

What are some current "idolatries" in the way we live and work?

. . . The blacksmith takes a tool and works with it in the coals; he shapes an idol with hammers, he forges it with the might of his arm. He gets hungry and loses his strength; he drinks no water and grows faint. The carpenter measures with a line and makes an outline with a marker; he roughs it out with chisels and marks it with compasses. He shapes it in the form of man, of man in all his glory, that it may dwell in a shrine. He cut down cedars, or perhaps took a cypress or oak. He let it grow among the trees of the forest, or planted a pine, and the rain made it grow. It is man's fuel for burning; some of it he takes and warms himself, he kindles a fire and bakes bread. But he also fashions a god and worships it; he makes an idol and bows down to it. Half of the wood he burns in the fire; over it he prepares his meal, he roasts his meat and eats his fill. He also warms himself and says, "Ah! I am warm; I see the fire." From the rest he makes a god, his idol; he bows down to it and worships. He prays to it and says, "Save me; you are my god." They know nothing, they understand nothing; their eyes are plastered over so they cannot see, and their minds closed so they cannot understand. No one stops to think, no one has the knowledge or understanding to say, "Half of it I used for fuel; I even baked bread over its coals, I roasted meat and I ate. Shall I make a detestable thing from what is left? Shall I bow down to a block of wood?" He feeds on ashes, a deluded heart misleads him; he cannot save himself, or say, "Is not this thing in my right hand a lie?"

EZEKIEL 28:5 (ABOUT THE CITY OF TYRE)

By your great skill in trading you have increased your wealth, and because of your wealth your heart has grown proud.

MARK 8:36

What good is it for a man to gain the whole world, yet forfeit his soul?

REVELATION 18:11–13 (ABOUT BABYLON)

The merchants of the earth will weep and mourn over her because no one buys their cargoes any more—cargoes of gold, silver, precious stones and pearls; fine linen, purple, silk and scarlet cloth; every sort of citron wood, and articles of every kind made of ivory, costly wood, bronze, iron and marble; cargoes of cinnamon and spice, of incense, myrrh and frankincense, of wine and olive oil, of fine flour and wheat; cattle and sheep; horses and carriages; and bodies and souls of men.

Questions

1. Take Jesus' question in Mark 8:36 above and reflect on what God might say to you through this warning.

2. Which of the comparisons in the following list are instructive for you as you think about God's designs vs. the Fall?

    - Work vs. Toil
    - Creativity vs. Necessity
    - Variety vs. Monotony
    - Purpose vs. Function
    - Tools vs. Machines
    - Multiplication vs. Repetition

3. Has the mechanization of work dehumanized us or improved our lives?

4. What factors might make some occupations unacceptable for a follower of Jesus Christ?

Why does some work seem futile? Because we are mortal. Why is work often so harsh and difficult? Because our sin brought "painful toil" on us.

If the story were to stop here, we would be trapped. The Gospel, however, offers an escape from our daily drudgery. Because of Jesus, we see eternity. As section 3 will reveal, we are able to recover substantially from the effects of sin.

Section Notes

SECTION 3
Restoring Work and the Worker

In section 1, we marveled at the panorama of God's workmanship and at his job description for us. In section 2, we were confronted with toil and futility—the existential struggle which results from sin. Can both be true? What is the synthesis? Here, we discover that Jesus Christ restored dignity to work and restored significance to us as workers. Hope returns.

"Because of his great love for us, God, who is rich in mercy, made us alive in Christ even when we were dead in transgressions—it is by grace you have been saved" (Ephesians 2:4–5).

This salvation has an effect, here and now, because it allows us to recover and restore meaning to what we do. Because we are committed to Christ, we are also committed to work with a purpose, knowing this: "Therefore, my dear brothers, stand firm. Let nothing move you. Always give yourselves fully to the work of the Lord, because you know that your labor in the Lord is not in vain" (1 Corinthians 15:58).

12

The Scriptures have some surprises for us when it comes to our values. We have wants and worries, priorities and possessions. How does Jesus challenge our conventional value system and, therefore, our reasons for work?

MATTHEW 6:25–34

Therefore I tell you, do not worry about your life, what you will eat or drink; or about your body, what you will wear. Is not life more important than food, and the body more important than clothes? Look at the birds of the air; they do not sow or reap or store away in barns, and yet your heavenly Father feeds them. Are you not much more valuable than they? Who of you by worrying can add a single hour to his life?

And why do you worry about clothes? See how the lilies of the field grow. They do not labor or spin. Yet I tell you that not even Solomon in all his splendor was dressed like one of these. If that is how God clothes the grass of the field, which is here today and tomorrow is thrown into the fire, will he not much more clothe you, O you of little faith? So do not worry, saying, 'What shall we eat?' or 'What shall we drink?' or 'What shall we wear?' For the pagans run after all these things, and your heavenly Father knows that you need them. But seek first his kingdom and his righteousness, and all these things will be given to you as well. Therefore do not worry about tomorrow, for tomorrow will worry about itself. Each day has enough trouble of its own.

The church . . . has allowed work and religion to become separate departments, and is astonished to find that, as a result, the secular work of the world is turned to purely selfish and destructive ends, and that the greater part of the world's intelligent workers have become irreligious or, at least, uninterested in religion.

Dorothy L. Sayers

JOHN 5:16–23

So, because Jesus was doing these things on the Sabbath, the Jews persecuted him. Jesus said to them, "My Father is always at his work to this very day, and I, too, am working." For this reason the Jews tried all the harder to kill him; not only was he breaking the Sabbath, but he was even calling God his own Father, making himself equal with God.

Jesus gave them this answer: "I tell you the truth, the Son can do nothing by himself; he can do only what he sees his Father doing, because whatever the Father does the Son also does. For the Father loves the Son and shows him all he does. Yes, to your amazement he will show him even greater things than these. For just as the Father raises the dead and gives them life, even so the Son gives life to whom he is pleased to give it. Moreover, the Father judges no one, but has entrusted all judgment to the Son, that all may honor the Son just as they honor the Father. He who does not honor the Son does not honor the Father, who sent him."

The Gospel of the kingdom orients us toward the lordship of Christ in every area of life: education, business, the arts, family, leisure, and politics. It embraces both creation and redemption: the present is building on the past . . . the future is breaking into the present. As Paul Stevens said, "Daily life is bursting with theological meaning."

JOHN 6:27–29

Do not work for food that spoils, but for food that endures to eternal life, which the Son of Man will give you. On him God the Father has placed his seal of approval. Then they asked him, "What must we do to do the works God requires?"

Jesus answered, "The work of God is this: to believe in the one he has sent."

> Work, for most of us, determines a great part of our opportunity for significance and the amount of good we are able to produce in a lifetime. Besides, work takes up so many of our waking hours that our jobs come to define us and give us our identities. We become what we do. Calling reverses such thinking. A sense of calling should precede a choice of job and career, and the main way to discover calling is along the lines of what we are each created and gifted to be. Instead of, 'You are what you do,' calling says: 'Do what you are.'
>
> *Os Guinness*

JOHN 17:1–5

After Jesus said this, he looked toward heaven and prayed: "Father, the time has come. Glorify your Son, that your Son may glorify you. For you granted him authority over all people that he might give eternal life to all those you have given him. Now this is eternal life: that they may know you, the only true God, and Jesus Christ, whom you have sent. I have brought you glory on earth by completing the work you gave me to do. And now, Father, glorify me in your presence with the glory I had with you before the world began."

Questions

1. How do Jesus' words transform your values and attitudes toward work?

2. The citizens of God's kingdom have an eternal perspective. How does this help us transcend the futility we experience?

Jesus Christ is the point of integration for us. He alone resolves our tensions that originated as a result of sin. "In him all things hold together" (Colossians 1:17b). Now, for us, the thorns and thistles still exist, but we can rejoin God as his co-laborers. Through the good news of the kingdom, we can enjoy a new scenario.

We can be wise, building our house on the rock of Jesus Christ by putting into practice what he has taught (Matthew 7:24). Our work shares in the redemption that is offered in Christ because there is new meaning in everything that is done as unto him.

13 What does it mean to work with God for his purposes?

1 CORINTHIANS 10:31
So whether you eat or drink or whatever you do, do it all for the glory of God.

We are kingdom people. We want to be in the world as salt: scattered, engaged, relevant, restorative. We should aim to be quality leaders as well as moral leaders. "Let us not become weary in doing good, for at the proper time we will reap a harvest if we do not give up" (Galatians 6:9).

---

1 CORINTHIANS 15:56–58

The sting of death is sin, and the power of sin is the law. But thanks be to God! He gives us the victory through our Lord Jesus Christ.

Therefore, my dear brothers, stand firm. Let nothing move you. Always give yourselves fully to the work of the Lord, because you know that your labor in the Lord is not in vain.

COLOSSIANS 3:17

And whatever you do, whether in word or deed, do it all in the name of the Lord Jesus, giving thanks to God the Father through him.

Questions

1. Summarize and reflect on how this understanding gives new insight into your responsibilities.

If God has called us to work, he has also supplied us with the resources to fulfill his calling. Shortage and scarcity are not his will. In our dependence upon him, we need to develop an "abundance mentality" without falling prey to spiritual consumerism.

14 In the context of daily life, the following scriptures reveal more of God's perspective on work. Look for the main points.

EXODUS 31:1–11

Then the LORD said to Moses, "See, I have chosen Bezalel son of Uri, the son of Hur, of the tribe of Judah, and I have filled him with the Spirit of God, with skill, ability and knowledge in all kinds of crafts—to make artistic designs for work in gold, silver and bronze, to cut and set stones, to work in wood, and to engage in all kinds of craftsmanship. Moreover, I have appointed Oholiab son of Ahisamach, of the tribe of Dan, to help him. Also I have given skill to all the craftsmen to make everything I have commanded you: the Tent of Meeting, the ark of the Testimony with the atonement cover on it, and all the other furnishings of the tent—the table and its articles, the pure gold lampstand and all its accessories, the altar of incense, the altar of burnt offering and all its utensils, the basin with its stand—and also the woven garments, both the sacred garments for Aaron the priest and the garments for his sons when they serve as priests, and the anointing oil and fragrant incense for the Holy Place. They are to make them just as I commanded you."

DEUTERONOMY 8:1–20

Be careful to follow every command I am giving you today, so that you may live and increase and may enter and possess the land that the LORD promised on oath to your forefathers. Remember how the LORD your God led you all the way in the desert these forty years, to humble you and to test you in order to know what was in your heart, whether or not you would keep his commands. He humbled you, causing you to hunger and then feeding you with manna, which neither you nor your fathers had known, to teach you that man does not live on bread alone but on every word that comes from the mouth of the LORD. Your clothes did not wear out and your feet did not swell during these forty years. Know then in your heart that as a man disciplines his son, so the LORD your God disciplines you. . . .

Work is not, primarily, a thing one does to live, but the thing one lives to do. It is, or it should be, the full expression of the worker's faculties, the thing in which he finds spiritual, mental, and bodily satisfaction, as the medium in which he offers himself to God.

Dorothy Sayers

... Observe the commands of the LORD your God, walking in his ways and revering him. For the LORD your God is bringing you into a good land—a land with streams and pools of water, with springs flowing in the valleys and hills; a land with wheat and barley, vines and fig trees, pomegranates, olive oil and honey; a land where bread will not be scarce and you will lack nothing; a land where the rocks are iron and you can dig copper out of the hills. ...

At Ben & Jerry's we see our bottom line as having two parts: how much financial profit we've made and how much of a contribution we have made to the community. A business that isn't profitable is financially bankrupt, but a business that isn't making a contribution to the community is morally bankrupt.

Ben Cohen, Co-founder of Ben & Jerry's Ice Cream

... When you have eaten and are satisfied, praise the LORD your God for the good land he has given you. Be careful that you do not forget the LORD your God, failing to observe his commands, his laws and his decrees that I am giving you this day. Otherwise, when you eat and are satisfied, when you build fine houses and settle down, and when your herds and flocks grow large and your silver and gold increase and all you have is multiplied, then your heart will become proud and you will forget the LORD your God, who brought you out of Egypt, out of the land of slavery. He led you through the vast and dreadful desert, that thirsty and waterless land, with its venomous snakes and scorpions. He brought you water out of hard rock. He gave you manna to eat in the desert, something your fathers had never known, to humble and to test you so that in the end it might go well with you. You may say to yourself, "My power and the strength of my hands have produced this wealth for me." But remember the LORD your God, for it is he who gives you the ability to produce wealth, and so confirms his covenant, which he swore to your forefathers, as it is today.

If you ever forget the LORD your God and follow other gods and worship and bow down to them, I testify against you today that you will surely be destroyed. Like the nations the LORD destroyed before you, so you will be destroyed for not obeying the LORD your God.

> I simply argue that the cross be raised again at the center of the marketplace as well as on the steeple of the church. I am recovering the claim that Jesus was not crucified in a cathedral between two candles, but on a cross between two thieves; on the town garbage heap; at a crossroad so cosmopolitan that they had to write his title in Hebrew and Latin and Greek . . . at the kind of place where cynics talk smut and thieves curse and soldiers gamble.
>
> *George MacLeod*

PROVERBS 31:10–31

A wife of noble character who can find? She is worth far more than rubies. Her husband has full confidence in her and lacks nothing of value. She brings him good, not harm, all the days of her life. She selects wool and flax and works with eager hands. She is like the merchant ships, bringing her food from afar. She gets up while it is still dark; she provides food for her family and portions for her servant girls. She considers a field and buys it; out of her earnings she plants a vineyard. She sets about her work vigorously; her arms are strong for her tasks. She sees that her trading is profitable, and her lamp does not go out at night. In her hand she holds the distaff and grasps the spindle with her fingers. She opens her arms to the poor and extends her hands to the needy. When it snows, she has no fear for her household; for all of them are clothed in scarlet. She makes coverings for her bed; she is clothed in fine linen and purple. Her husband is respected at the city gate, where he takes his seat among the elders of the land. She makes linen garments and sells them, and supplies the merchants with sashes. She is clothed with strength and dignity; she can laugh at the days to come. She speaks with wisdom, and faithful instruction is on her tongue. She watches over the affairs of her household and does not eat the bread of idleness. Her children arise and call her blessed; her husband also, and he praises her: "Many women do noble things, but you surpass them all." Charm is deceptive, and beauty is fleeting; but a woman who fears the LORD is to be praised. Give her the reward she has earned, and let her works bring her praise at the city gate.

> Half of the pleasure from the business calling derives from a sense that the system of which it is a part is highly beneficial to the human race, morally sound, and one of the great social achievements of all time. The other half is personal—finding purpose and meaning in what one does.
>
> *Michael Novak*

ECCLESIASTES 3:9–14

What does the worker gain from his toil? I have seen the burden God has laid on men. He has made everything beautiful in its time. He has also set eternity in the hearts of men; yet they cannot fathom what God has done from beginning to end. I know that there is nothing better for men than to be happy and do good while they live. That everyone may eat and drink, and find satisfaction in all his toil—this is the gift of God. I know that everything God does will endure forever; nothing can be added to it and nothing taken from it. God does it so that men will revere him.

All our merely natural activities will be accepted, if they are offered to God, even the humblest. And all of them, even the noblest, will be sinful if they are not.

C.S. Lewis

ISAIAH 58:6–12

Is not this the kind of fasting I have chosen: to loose the chains of injustice and untie the cords of the yoke, to set the oppressed free and break every yoke? Is it not to share your food with the hungry and to provide the poor wanderer with shelter—when you see the naked, to clothe him, and not to turn away from your own flesh and blood? Then your light will break forth like the dawn, and your healing will quickly appear; then your righteousness will go before you, and the glory of the LORD will be your rear guard. Then you will call, and the LORD will answer; you will cry for help, and he will say: Here am I.

If you do away with the yoke of oppression, with the pointing finger and malicious talk, and if you spend yourselves in behalf of the hungry and satisfy the needs of the oppressed, then your light will rise in the darkness, and your night will become like the noonday. The LORD will guide you always; he will satisfy your needs in a sun-scorched land and will strengthen your frame. You will be like a well-watered garden, like a spring whose waters never fail. Your people will rebuild the ancient ruins and will raise up the age-old foundations; you will be called Repairer of Broken Walls, Restorer of Streets with Dwellings.

Work will be part of our participation in the "new heavens and new earth." God tells us—"they will build houses and dwell in them; they will plant vineyards and eat their fruit. No longer will they build houses and others live in them, or plant and others eat. . . . My chosen ones will long enjoy the works of their hands. They will not toil in vain. . . ." (Isaiah 65:21–23). So we see that futility will be banished . . . and our anonymous modern gaps between producers and consumers will evaporate.

ISAIAH 61:1–4

The Spirit of the Sovereign LORD is on me, because the LORD has anointed me to preach good news to the poor. He has sent me to bind up the brokenhearted, to proclaim freedom for the captives and release from darkness for the prisoners, to proclaim the year of the LORD'S favor and the day of vengeance of our God, to comfort all who mourn, and provide for those who grieve in Zion—to bestow on them a crown of beauty instead of ashes, the oil of gladness instead of mourning, and a garment of praise instead of a spirit of despair. They will be called oaks of righteousness, a planting of the LORD for the display of his splendor. They will rebuild the ancient ruins and restore the places long devastated; they will renew the ruined cities that have been devastated for generations.

Questions

1. What should be the focus of our work?

2. Should we expect fulfillment from our work? Why or why not?

3. What are some criteria for making our work pleasing to God?

4. How would you advise a fellow employee who is frustrated and wants to be "used by God"?

15 Does God provide for our needs? Or does God hold us responsible to provide for ourselves and our families? Reflect on that tension in the light of the following scriptures.

MATTHEW 6:33–34

But seek first his kingdom and his righteousness, and all these things will be given to you as well. Therefore do not worry about tomorrow, for tomorrow will worry about itself. Each day has enough trouble of its own.

> As Christians in business, our mission is to honor God in the world of work and economics by extending his reign to all our activities. With Jesus as Lord of the marketplace, our task is to love, serve, preach, and heal. We use our faith, skills and resources to correct inequities, work toward economic justice, seek righteousness, bring hope where there is not hope, and make all things new.
>
> *Mennonite Economic Development Associates*

ACTS 20:33–35

I have not coveted anyone's silver or gold or clothing. You yourselves know that these hands of mine have supplied my own needs and the needs of my companions. In everything I did, I showed you that by this kind of hard work we must help the weak, remembering the words the Lord Jesus himself said: 'It is more blessed to give than to receive.'

> We must neither succumb to passivity at work nor a "welfare complex" nor elbow God out of the way in pursuit of our own agendas.

2 THESSALONIANS 3:6–12

In the name of the Lord Jesus Christ, we command you, brothers, to keep away from every brother who is idle and does not live according to the teaching you received from us. For you yourselves know how you ought to follow our example. We were not idle when we were with you, nor did we eat anyone's food without paying for it. On the contrary, we worked night and day, laboring and toiling so that we would not be a burden to any of you. We did this, not because we do not have the right to such help, but in order to make ourselves a model for you to follow. For even when we were with you, we gave you this rule: "If a man will not work, he shall not eat."

We hear that some among you are idle. They are not busy; they are busybodies. Such people we command and urge in the Lord Jesus Christ to settle down and earn the bread they eat.

Questions

1. How should we work in light of our role and our need for God?

16 In Acts 10:38, we are told that "Jesus . . . went around doing good." What did he do and why was it good? In the New Testament, "good works" are frequently mentioned.

2 CORINTHIANS 9:6–8

Remember this: Whoever sows sparingly will also reap sparingly, and whoever sows generously will also reap generously. Each man should give what he has decided in his heart to give, not reluctantly or under compulsion, for God loves a cheerful giver. And God is able to make all grace abound to you, so that in all things at all times, having all that you need, you will abound in every good work.

> Good works in the Scriptures can relate to morality and charity and productivity. They embrace occupations, deeds, and accomplishments . . . as we exercise our creativity in serving people and strengthening the world.

EPHESIANS 2:10

For we are God's workmanship, created in Christ Jesus to do good works, which God prepared in advance for us to do.

1 TIMOTHY 6:17–19

Command those who are rich in this present world not to be arrogant nor to put their hope in wealth, which is so uncertain, but to put their hope in God, who richly provides us with everything for our enjoyment. Command them to do good, to be rich in good deeds, and to be generous and willing to share. In this way they will lay up treasure for themselves as a firm foundation for the coming age, so that they may take hold of the life that is truly life.

2 TIMOTHY 3:16–17

All Scripture is God-breathed and is useful for teaching, rebuking, correcting and training in righteousness, so that the man of God may be thoroughly equipped for every good work.

Questions

1. What are some examples of "good works" in your life?

2. Do you experience joy in knowing that your professional work, when done well and in faith, is indeed a form of "good works" in God's eyes?

17 How does attitude affect work?

PSALM 128:1–4
Blessed are all who fear the LORD, who walk in his ways. You will eat the fruit of your labor; blessings and prosperity will be yours. Your wife will be like a fruitful vine within your house; your sons will be like olive shoots around your table. Thus is the man blessed who fears the LORD.

1 CORINTHIANS 4:2
Now it is required that those who have been given a trust must prove faithful.

1 CORINTHIANS 7:29–31
What I mean, brothers, is that the time is short. From now on those who have wives should live as if they had none; those who mourn, as if they did not; those who are happy, as if they were not; those who buy something, as if it were not theirs to keep; those who use the things of the world, as if not engrossed in them. For this world in its present form is passing away.

Following the teachings of the Bible, "Luther placed a crown on the sweaty forehead of labor."

Adriano Tilgher

COLOSSIANS 3:17
And whatever you do, whether in word or deed, do it all in the name of the Lord Jesus, giving thanks to God the Father through him.

1 THESSALONIANS 1:2–3

We always thank God for all of you, mentioning you in our prayers. We continually remember before our God and Father your work produced by faith, your labor prompted by love, and your endurance inspired by hope in our Lord Jesus Christ.

> The basis for determining the value of human work is not primarily the kind of work being done, but the fact that the one who is doing it is a person. . . . Such a concept does away with the ancient differentiation of people into classes according to the kind of work done. . . . In the first place, work is for man and not man for work.
>
> *Pope John Paul II*

COLOSSIANS 3:22–25

Slaves, obey your earthly masters in everything; and do it, not only when their eye is on you and to win their favor, but with sincerity of heart and reverence for the Lord. Whatever you do, work at it with all your heart, as working for the Lord, not for men, since you know that you will receive an inheritance from the Lord as a reward. It is the Lord Christ you are serving. Anyone who does wrong will be repaid for his wrong, and there is no favoritism.

Questions

1. How do our perspectives about work affect our attitudes?

2. Which positive attitudes are most lacking in the workplace and how should we promote them?

The workplace is rife with relational tensions, moral dilemmas, and personal and professional frustrations. It is a complex environment. A godly attitude helps us balance and control these inevitable tensions.

18. The Book of Proverbs provides practical principles for daily life. Consider the following proverbs and then summarize what they tell us about work.

Lazy hands make a man poor, but diligent hands bring wealth. (10:4)

The man of integrity walks securely, but he who takes crooked paths will be found out. (10:9)

The LORD abhors dishonest scales, but accurate weights are his delight. (11:1)

He who works his land will have abundant food, but he who chases fantasies lacks judgment. (12:11)

All hard work brings a profit, but mere talk leads only to poverty. (14:23)

He who oppresses the poor shows contempt for their Maker, but whoever is kind to the needy honors God. (14:31)

Plans fail for lack of counsel, but with many advisers they succeed. (15:22)

Commit to the LORD whatever you do, and your plans will succeed. (16:3)

Honest scales and balances are from the LORD; all the weights in the bag are of his making. (16:11)

One who is slack in his work is brother to one who destroys. (18:9)

---

*Are we to assess people by their level of income?
If not, what do varieties in wages signify?*

The sluggard's craving will be the death of him, because his hands refuse to work. (21:25)

Do you see a man skilled in his work? He will serve before kings; he will not serve before obscure men. (22:29)

Do not wear yourself out to get rich; have the wisdom to show restraint. (23:4)

Finish your outdoor work and get your fields ready; after that, build your house. (24:27)

Be sure you know the condition of your flocks, give careful attention to your herds. (27:23)

Keep falsehood and lies far from me; give me neither poverty nor riches, but give me only my daily bread. Otherwise, I may have too much and disown you and say, 'Who is the LORD?' Or I may become poor and steal, and so dishonor the name of my God. (30:8–9)

Questions

1. Summarize what these proverbs tell us about work.
2. List some practical ideas for how to change behavior in the marketplace.

19 From the following scriptures, identify several ways in which we need to grow and develop as workers.

PROVERBS 1:1–5

The proverbs of Solomon son of David, king of Israel: for attaining wisdom and discipline; for understanding words of insight; for acquiring a disciplined and prudent life, doing what is right and just and fair; for giving prudence to the simple, knowledge and discretion to the young—let the wise listen and add to their learning, and let the discerning get guidance...

MICAH 6:8

And what does the Lord require of you? To act justly and to love mercy and to walk humbly with your God.

> Micah's threefold test applies to those of us whom God has placed in management roles today. These three statements of responsibility... do justice, love mercy, walk humbly with your God... are demands that Christian managers should be using to measure each business decision they make, especially in the context of its impact on their employees.

ROMANS 12:1–2

Therefore, I urge you, brothers, in view of God's mercy, to offer your bodies as living sacrifices, holy and pleasing to God—this is your spiritual act of worship. Do not conform any longer to the pattern of this world, but be transformed by the renewing of your mind. Then you will be able to test and approve what God's will is—his good, pleasing and perfect will.

1 CORINTHIANS 9:24–27

Do you not know that in a race all the runners run, but only one gets the prize? Run in such a way as to get the prize. Everyone who competes in the games goes into strict training. They do it to get a crown that will not last; but we do it to get a crown that will last forever. Therefore I do not run like a man running aimlessly; I do not fight like a man beating the air. No, I beat my body and make it my slave so that after I have preached to others, I myself will not be disqualified for the prize.

HEBREWS 12:1–3

Therefore, since we are surrounded by such a great cloud of witnesses, let us throw off everything that hinders and the sin that so easily entangles, and let us run with perseverance the race marked out for us. Let us fix our eyes on Jesus, the author and perfecter of our faith, who for the joy set before him endured the cross, scorning its shame, and sat down at the right hand of the throne of God. Consider him who endured such opposition from sinful men, so that you will not grow weary and lose heart.

Today we have become deaf to what Martin Luther described as the "calling." ... Shall we opt for a quality brand or shall we settle for a vacuous label that only delivers unhappiness, an empty exercise in gratification?

Richard Donkin

JAMES 1:2-4

Consider it pure joy, my brothers, whenever you face trials of many kinds, because you know that the testing of your faith develops perseverance. Perseverance must finish its work so that you may be mature and complete, not lacking anything.

Questions

1. Which of these activities or commitments stand out as necessary for you in your circumstances?

2. How would you counsel a fellow employee who feels that his or her work is futile?

3. What actions are unacceptable for a believer in the workplace?

Review the practical ways in which the Scriptures can help you to "be transformed by the renewing of your mind" (Romans 12:2). God was pleased, through Jesus Christ, "to reconcile to himself all things" (Colossians 1:20). Work, therefore, has been more than "redefined." It is restored so that our perspective on work is forever changed because we know that our Lord dignified and enhanced human work.

Next, in section 4, we will consider how to integrate our view of work, especially around the idea of service.

Section Notes

SECTION 4
Work as Service

One of the core cultural presuppositions of our times is rooted in radical individualism. We believe that life is about me, myself, and I. Early signs of this view appear in literary history. The famous poet Walt Whitman wrote a blatantly egotistical poem in the 1800s titled, appropriately, *Song of Myself*. It is an ode to individualism that is 1346 lines long! As an example of its narcissism, one stanza says: "I hear and behold God in every object, yet undersand God not in the least. Nor do I understand who there can be more wonderful than myself."

It would be naive to think that the individualism of our culture hasn't affected our view of work in ways that distort God's original designs for our lives. And here the Scriptures completely contradict what the world imposes on us. As we will see, the meaning of life is actually found in being selfless. We find life by serving others.

In this section, we will explore what God expects of us in our work. What is our service to God and others, and how do we pursue it?

20. A constant tension for most of us lies in how to integrate all the competing elements of life. We still feel "compartmentalized." How do the following scriptures demonstrate integration?

MATTHEW 22:37–40

Jesus replied: "'Love the Lord your God with all your heart and with all your soul and with all your mind.' This is the first and greatest commandment. And the second is like it: 'Love your neighbor as yourself.' All the Law and the Prophets hang on these two commandments."

> A disciple of Jesus Christ should be an "amateur," in the root sense of this term; namely, one who acts out of love rather than because of some professional obligation.

MATTHEW 25:31–40

When the Son of Man comes in his glory, and all the angels with him, he will sit on his throne in heavenly glory. All the nations will be gathered before him, and he will separate the people one from another as a shepherd separates the sheep from the goats. He will put the sheep on his right and the goats on his left.

Then the King will say to those on his right, 'Come, you who are blessed by my Father; take your inheritance, the kingdom prepared for you since the creation of the world. For I was hungry and you gave me something to eat, I was thirsty and you gave me something to drink, I was a stranger and you invited me in, I needed clothes and you clothed me, I was sick and you looked after me, I was in prison and you came to visit me.'

Then the righteous will answer him, 'Lord, when did we see you hungry and feed you, or thirsty and give you something to drink? When did we see you a stranger and invite you in, or needing clothes and clothe you? When did we see you sick or in prison and go to visit you?'

The King will reply, 'I tell you the truth, whatever you did for one of the least of these brothers of mine, you did for me.'

The Bible teaches . . . that we should plan and live our life as a unity in which nothing is secular and everything is in a real sense sacred, because everything is being done for the glory of God—that is, to show appreciation for what he has made, to please him by loving obedience to his commands, and to advance his honor and praise among his creatures, starting with the homage and adoration that we render to him ourselves. Nothing is to be viewed as less than sacred; there is to be no compartmentalizing of our daily doings; work is to be a unifying reality that holds all our life together.

J.I. Packer

---

1 JOHN 4:10–11, 19–21

This is love: not that we loved God, but that he loved us and sent his Son as an atoning sacrifice for our sins. Dear friends, since God so loved us, we also ought to love one another.

We love because he first loved us. If anyone says, "I love God," yet hates his brother, he is a liar. For anyone who does not love his brother, whom he has seen, cannot love God, whom he has not seen. And he has given us this command: Whoever loves God must also love his brother.

Questions

1. How do these scriptures combine our two primary responsibilities (to serve God and others)?

Occasionally, translations of the Scriptures conceal part of the truth that is being expressed. There is an instructive example in Acts 6 where the Greek noun *diakonia* and verb *diakoneo* are translated, within the space of only four verses, as distribute... wait on... minister. In addition, some translations, such as the NIV, insert "the ministry of" in verse 2, where it does not occur in the Greek original.

Does this matter? Yes, because the effect is to reinforce a common prejudice that some activities are "ministry" and some are not. *Diakonia* simply means service.

21 Read these four verses and look carefully at how the Greek term is used.

ACTS 6:1–4

In those days when the number of disciples was increasing, the Grecian Jews among them complained against the Hebraic Jews because their widows were being overlooked in the daily distribution (*diakonia*) of food. So the Twelve gathered all the disciples together and said, "It would not be right for us to neglect the ministry (not in the Greek) of the word of God in order to wait on (*diakoneo*) tables. Brothers, choose seven men from among you who are known to be full of the Spirit and wisdom. We will turn this responsibility over to them and will give our attention to prayer and the ministry (*diakonia*) of the word."

Questions

1. What does this tell us about what we often call "ministry"?
2. What are the qualifications for "waiting on tables" in verse 3?
3. What is the relationship between "work" and "ministry"?
4. Is there a hierarchy of work in which some jobs are more "spiritual" than others?

We should not conclude that to be a professional religious worker is an inferior occupation. Such people are often set apart "so that the Body of Christ may be built up" (Ephesians 4:12). However, their functions do not mean that they become a special caste or elite.

22 The basic Greek term for work (*ergon*) and the related verb cover a wide range of activities. Note how it is used in the following scriptures.

LUKE 13:14

Indignant because Jesus had healed on the Sabbath, the synagogue ruler said to the people, "There are six days for work (*ergon*). So come and be healed on those days, not on the Sabbath."

JOHN 4:34

"My food," said Jesus, "is to do the will of him who sent me and to finish his work (*ergon*)."

The Church's approach to an intelligent carpenter is usually confined to exhorting him not to be drunk and disorderly in his leisure hours, and to come to church on Sundays. What the Church should be telling him is this: that the very first demand that his religion makes upon him is that he should make good tables. . . .

Every maker and worker is called to serve God in his profession or trade—not outside it. . . . Let the Church see to it that the workers are Christian people and do their work well, as to God: then all the work will be Christian work, whether it is Church embroidery, or sewage-farming.

Dorothy Sayers

EPHESIANS 4:12

To prepare God's people for works (*ergon*) of service (*diakonia*), so that the body of Christ may be built up.

1 THESSALONIANS 4:11

Make it your ambition to lead a quiet life, to mind your own business and to work (*ergon*) with your hands, just as we told you.

HEBREWS 6:10

God is not unjust; he will not forget your work (*ergon*) and the love you have shown him as you have helped his people and continue to help them.

Questions

1. Some have observed that to speak of the "sacred" and the "secular" makes an unbiblical distinction. In light of what you have studied, do you agree with this? Why or why not?

In Matthew 25:14–30, Jesus tells us what the kingdom of heaven will be like. The immediate focus is the use of money, but the principles are wider. Money and property (v. 14-15) are used to illustrate the reality that we have differing levels of resources, ability, and capacity. Indeed, here is an application of God's mandate that we "be fruitful . . . subdue . . . rule over," in Genesis 1:28.

23 As you read Genesis 1:28 and the story from Matthew 25, make notes in order to answer the first question below.

GENESIS 1:28

God blessed them and said to them, "Be fruitful and increase in number; fill the earth and subdue it. Rule over the fish of the sea and the birds of the air and over every living creature that moves on the ground."

When work began to be viewed in primarily economic terms with the arrival of the Industrial Revolution, it became customary to look upon work as something the worker owns and sells to the highest bidder. As alternatives to that view, capitalism often operates on the premise that the employer owns the work of people (since work is a means of production), while socialism operates on the premise that society owns work. But the Christian view of the worker as steward suggests something truly revolutionary: God is the rightful owner of human work. . . . Work can be redeemed from many of the effects of the Fall. The key elements in that redemption are a realization that common work in the world bears God's approval, the belief that God calls us to our work, and an awareness that we are stewards who serve God with the work he has entrusted to us.

Leland Ryken

MATTHEW 25:14–30

Again, it will be like a man going on a journey, who called his servants and entrusted his property to them. To one he gave five talents of money, to another two talents, and to another one talent, each according to his ability. Then he went on his journey. The man who had received the five talents went at once and put his money to work and gained five more. So also, the one with the two talents gained two more. But the man who had received the one talent went off, dug a hole in the ground and hid his master's money.

After a long time the master of those servants returned and settled accounts with them. The man who had received the five talents brought the other five. 'Master,' he said, 'you entrusted me with five talents. See, I have gained five more.'

His master replied, 'Well done, good and faithful servant! You have been faithful with a few things; I will put you in charge of many things. Come and share your master's happiness!'

The man with the two talents also came. 'Master,' he said, 'you entrusted me with two talents; see, I have gained two more.'

His master replied, 'Well done, good and faithful servant! You have been faithful with a few things; I will put you in charge of many things. Come and share your master's happiness!'

Then the man who had received the one talent came. 'Master,' he said, 'I knew that you are a hard man, harvesting where you have not sown and gathering where you have not scattered seed. So I was afraid and went out and hid your talent in the ground. See, here is what belongs to you.'

His master replied, 'You wicked, lazy servant! So you knew that I harvest where I have not sown and gather where I have not scattered seed? Well then, you should have put my money on deposit with the bankers, so that when I returned I would have received it back with interest.

'Take the talent from him and give it to the one who has the ten talents. For everyone who has will be given more, and he will have an abundance. Whoever does not have, even what he has will be taken from him. And throw that worthless servant outside, into the darkness, where there will be weeping and gnashing of teeth.'

Questions

1. Based on the above scriptures, complete these statements:

   Work is owned by . . .

   God expects . . .

   Work is the responsibility of . . .

   God judges . . .

   Faithfulness is identified as . . .

   God's approval results in . . .

2. Why do you think the servant who did not invest is called "wicked" (verse 26) as well as lazy? Did he sin or did he merely lack financial competence?

24 Work is part of God's purpose for us. Therefore, we must make energetic use of work opportunities through our stewardship of the skills and resources entrusted to us.

EPHESIANS 2:10

For we are God's workmanship, created in Christ Jesus to do good works, which God prepared in advance for us to do.

COLOSSIANS 3:23–24

Whatever you do, work at it with all your heart, as working for the Lord, not for men, since you know that you will receive an inheritance from the Lord as a reward. It is the Lord Christ you are serving.

2 TIMOTHY 2:20–21

In a large house there are articles not only of gold and silver, but also of wood and clay; some are for noble purposes and some for ignoble. If a man cleanses himself from the latter, he will be an instrument for noble purposes, made holy, useful to the Master and prepared to do any good work.

1 PETER 4:10–11

Each one should use whatever gift he has received to serve others, faithfully administering God's grace in its various forms. If anyone speaks, he should do it as one speaking the very words of God. If anyone serves, he should do it with the strength God provides, so that in all things God may be praised through Jesus Christ. To him be the glory and the power for ever and ever. Amen.

> Much religion has built on the idea that the material order ... is evil, and therefore to be refused and ignored as far as possible. This view, which dehumanizes its devotees, has sometimes called itself Christian, but it is really as un-Christian as can be. For matter, being made by God, was and is good in his eyes, and so should be so in ours. We serve God by using and enjoying temporal things gratefully, with a sense of their value to him their Maker, and of his generosity in giving them to us.
>
> *J.I. Packer*

Questions

1. What do the Scriptures suggest about our choice of work?
2. How should we integrate natural abilities, learned skills, and spiritual gifts with our understanding of what God asks us to do?

Suggestion: Prayerfully review the work to which you are currently committed. How can you align your practice and performance so as to be a "good and faithful servant" (Matthew 25:21–23)?

If you are called to be a street sweeper, sweep streets even as Michelangelo painted, or Beethoven composed music, or Shakespeare wrote poetry. Sweep streets so well that all the hosts of heaven and earth will pause to say, 'here lived a great street sweeper who did his job well.'

Martin Luther King, Jr.

Story 1: Creativity in the Workplace

About three weeks after I had spoken to three thousand employees of a large supermarket chain in the Midwest on coming up with their own creative personal signature, my phone rang late one afternoon. The person on the line told me that his name was Johnny and that he was a bagger at one of the stores. He also told me that he was a person with Down Syndrome. He said, "Barbara, I like what you said!" Then he went on to tell me that when he'd gone home the night of my presentation, he had asked his dad to teach him to use the computer.

He said they set it up in three columns, and each night now when he goes home, he finds a "good thought for the day." He said when he can't find one he likes, he "thinks one up!" Then he types it into the computer, prints out multiple copies, cuts them out and signs his name on the back of each one. The next day as he bags customers' groceries "with flourish," Johnny puts a thought for the day in each person's groceries, adding his own signature in a heartwarming, fun, and creative way.

One month later, the manager of the store called me. He said, "Barbara, you won't believe what happened today. When I went out on the floor this morning, the line at Johnny's checkout was three times longer than any other line! I went ballistic, yelling, 'Get more lanes open! Get more people out here!' but the customers said, 'No, no! We want to be in Johnny's lane—we want the thought for the day!'"

The manager said one woman even came up and told him, "I only used to shop once a week, and now I come here every time I go by because I want the thought for the day!" (Imagine what that does to the bottom line!) He ended by saying, "Who do you think is the most important person in our whole store?" Johnny, of course!

Three months later he called me again. "You and Johnny have

transformed our store! Now in the floral department when they have a broken flower or an unused corsage, they go out on the floor and find an elderly woman or a little girl and pin it on them. One of our meat packers loves Snoopy, so he bought fifty thousand Snoopy stickers, and each time he packages a piece of meat, he puts a Snoopy sticker on it. We are having so much fun, and our customers are having so much fun!" THAT is spirit in the workplace! (From "Developing Your Personal Signature" by Barbara Glanz, from the book *Heart at Work* by Jack Canfield and Jacqueline Miller.)

Questions

1. In the light of the above story, which creative services establish your identity as a contributor in your context?

Story 2: Genuine Concern in the Workplace

I do a lot of management training each year for Circle K Corporation, a national chain of convenience stores.

Among the topics we address in our seminars is the retention of quality employees, which is a real challenge to managers when considering the available pay scale in the service industry.

During these discussions, I ask the participants, "What has caused you to stay long enough to become a manager?" Some time back, a new manager took the question and responded slowly, her voice almost breaking; she said, "It was a $19 baseball glove."

Cynthia told the group that she originally took the Circle K clerk job as an interim position while she looked for better employment. On her second or third day behind the counter, she received a phone call from her nine-year-old son, Jessie. She explained that, as a single mother, money was very tight. She had to tell Jessie that her first check would have to be used for bills and that perhaps she could buy his little league glove with her second or third check.

When Cynthia arrived for work the next morning, Patricia, the store manager, asked her to come to the small room in the back of the store that served as an office. Cynthia thought perhaps she had done something wrong or left some part of her job incomplete from the day before. She was concerned and confused.

Cynthia then told us that Patricia had handed her a box and said, "I overheard you talking to your son yesterday and I know that it is hard to explain things to kids. This is a baseball glove for Jessie because he may not understand how important he is even though you have to pay bills before you can buy gloves. You know we can't pay good people like you as much as we would like to. But we do care and I want you to know you are important to us."

The story of the thoughtfulness, empathy, and love of a convenience store manager demonstrated vividly that people remember more about how an employer cares than about how an employer pays. An important lesson for the price of a little league baseball glove. (From "Jessie's Glove" by Rick Phillips, from the book *Heart at Work,* by Jack Canfield and Jacqueline Miller.)

Questions

1. What does this story reveal about lasting significance in our daily occupations?

Section Notes

SECTION 5
Rest and Recreation

God is interested in our overall well-being, not just our productivity. Rest, he declared, is holy. Even the aesthetic beauty of his creation is, in part, designed to enrich our lives. In our stressful, anxious, competitive times, we often attempt to find rest in activities that fail to truly enrich our souls. We need a true understanding of the place of rest in God's design.

25 What do the following scriptures tell us about God's purposes beyond the merely functional and utilitarian?

GENESIS 2:9
And the LORD God made all kinds of trees grow out of the ground—trees that were pleasing to the eye and good for food. In the middle of the garden were the tree of life and the tree of the knowledge of good and evil.

Earth's crammed with heaven, and every common bush afire with God; but only he who sees takes off his shoes.

Elizabeth Barrett Browning

---

1 CHRONICLES 28:11–12, 19–21

Then David gave his son Solomon the plans for the portico of the temple, its buildings, its storerooms, its upper parts, its inner rooms and the place of atonement. He gave him the plans of all that the Spirit had put in his mind for the courts of the temple of the LORD and all the surrounding rooms, for the treasuries of the temple of God and for the treasuries for the dedicated things.... "All this," David said, "I have in writing from the hand of the LORD upon me, and he gave me understanding in all the details of the plan...."

God wanted his house to be elaborate and of the highest quality, excellent in every detail.

... David also said to Solomon his son, "Be strong and courageous, and do the work. Do not be afraid or discouraged, for the LORD God, my God, is with you. He will not fail you or forsake you until all the work for the service of the temple of the LORD is finished. The divisions of the priests and Levites are ready for all the work on the temple of God, and every willing man skilled in any craft will help you in all the work. The officials and all the people will obey your every command."

2 CHRONICLES 30:21–27

The Israelites who were present in Jerusalem celebrated the Feast of Unleavened Bread for seven days with great rejoicing, while the Levites and priests sang to the LORD every day, accompanied by the LORD'S instruments of praise.

Hezekiah spoke encouragingly to all the Levites, who showed good understanding of the service of the LORD. For the seven days they ate their assigned portion and offered fellowship offerings and praised the LORD, the God of their fathers.

The whole assembly then agreed to celebrate the festival seven more days; so for another seven days they celebrated joyfully. Hezekiah king of Judah provided a thousand bulls and seven thousand sheep and goats for the assembly, and the officials provided them with a thousand bulls and ten thousand sheep and goats. A great number of priests consecrated themselves. The entire assembly of Judah rejoiced, along with the priests and Levites and all who had assembled from Israel, including the aliens who had come from Israel and those who lived in Judah. There was great joy in Jerusalem, for since the days of Solomon son of David king of Israel there had been nothing like this in Jerusalem. The priests and the Levites stood to bless the people, and God heard them, for their prayer reached heaven, his holy dwelling place.

Look at the motivation and outcome of your pleasures. How hard do you chase after them? What kind of behavior do they produce? What is your response to them when they come? If pleasure comes unsought, or as our grateful acceptance of a gift providentially set before us, and if the pleasure does no damage to ourselves or others, and if the delight of it prompts fresh thanksgiving to God, then it is holy.

J.I. Packer

ECCLESIASTES 5:18–19

Then I realized that it is good and proper for a man to eat and drink, and to find satisfaction in his toilsome labor under the sun during the few days of life God has given him—for this is his lot. Moreover, when God gives any man wealth and possessions, and enables him to enjoy them, to accept his lot and be happy in his work—this is a gift of God.

It's difficult to cultivate a sense of wonder in the workplace. Knowledge and competence are the key values here. We don't want any surprises. . . . Along the way, the primacy of God and his work gives way ever so slightly to the primacy of our work in God's kingdom. We begin to think of ways to use God in what we're doing. . . . It turns out that we have not so much been worshiping God as enlisting him as a trusted and valuable assistant.

Eugene Peterson

MATTHEW 6:28–29

And why do you worry about clothes? See how the lilies of the field grow. They do not labor or spin. Yet I tell you that not even Solomon in all his splendor was dressed like one of these.

The inner joyfulness of the person who is celebrating belongs to the very core of what we mean by leisure.... Leisure is only possible in the assumption that man is not only in harmony with himself, but also that he is in agreement with the world and its meaning. Leisure lives on affirmation. It is not the same as the absence of activity.

Josef Pieper

JOHN 2:1–11

On the third day a wedding took place at Cana in Galilee. Jesus' mother was there, and Jesus and his disciples had also been invited to the wedding. When the wine was gone, Jesus' mother said to him, "They have no more wine."

"Dear woman, why do you involve me?" Jesus replied. "My time has not yet come."

His mother said to the servants, "Do whatever he tells you."

Nearby stood six stone water jars, the kind used by the Jews for ceremonial washing, each holding from twenty to thirty gallons.

Jesus said to the servants, "Fill the jars with water"; so they filled them to the brim.

Then he told them, "Now draw some out and take it to the master of the banquet."

They did so, and the master of the banquet tasted the water that had been turned into wine. He did not realize where it had come from, though the servants who had drawn the water knew. Then he called the bridegroom aside and said, "Everyone brings out the choice wine first and then the cheaper wine after the guests have had too much to drink; but you have saved the best till now."

This, the first of his miraculous signs, Jesus performed at Cana in Galilee. He thus revealed his glory, and his disciples put their faith in him.

During this wedding celebration, Jesus makes lavish provision for the success of the party.

Questions

1. What does God's interest in aesthetics and pleasure say about rest?

26 In the Old Testament, God set apart the Sabbath for the Jews as a holy day. Sabbath simply means "rest." In the following scriptures, note the reasons for God's introduction of the Sabbath.

GENESIS 2:1–3

Thus the heavens and the earth were completed in all their vast array. By the seventh day God had finished the work he had been doing; so on the seventh day he rested from all his work. And God blessed the seventh day and made it holy, because on it he rested from all the work of creating that he had done.

The Hebrew word shabbat is linked to the verb sabat, which means to stop or cease. In Akkadian, sibbitim means seventh.

EXODUS 20:8–11

Remember the Sabbath day by keeping it holy. Six days you shall labor and do all your work, but the seventh day is a Sabbath to the LORD your God. On it you shall not do any work, neither you, nor your son or daughter, nor your manservant or maidservant, nor your animals, nor the alien within your gates. For in six days the LORD made the heavens and the earth, the sea, and all that is in them, but he rested on the seventh day. Therefore the LORD blessed the Sabbath day and made it holy.

There is a realm of time where the goal is not to have but to be, not to own but to give, not to control but to share, not to subdue but to be in accord.

Abraham Heschel

EXODUS 23:12

Six days do your work, but on the seventh day do not work, so that your ox and your donkey may rest and the slave born in your household, and the alien as well, may be refreshed.

EXODUS 34:21

... [E]ven during the plowing season and harvest, you must rest.

> Enslavement to activities is worldliness in its purest form: compulsive workaholism is as worldly as is any form of laziness. Whether persons are worldly or not depends not on how much pleasure they take from life, but on the spirit in which they take it. If we let pleasant things engross us so that we forget God, we are worldly.... Worldliness is the spirit that substitutes earthly goals (pleasure, profit, popularity, privilege, power) for life's true goal, which is the praise of God.
>
> J.I. Packer

LEVITICUS 25:1–7

The LORD said to Moses on Mount Sinai, "Speak to the Israelites and say to them: 'When you enter the land I am going to give you, the land itself must observe a sabbath to the LORD. For six years sow your fields, and for six years prune your vineyards and gather their crops. But in the seventh year the land is to have a sabbath of rest, a sabbath to the LORD. Do not sow your fields or prune your vineyards. Do not reap what grows of itself or harvest the grapes of your untended vines. The land is to have a year of rest. Whatever the land yields during the sabbath year will be food for you—for yourself, your manservant and maidservant, and the hired worker and temporary resident who live among you, as well as for your livestock and the wild animals in your land. Whatever the land produces may be eaten."

Our use of leisure always reflects our values.
A good leisure life:
- contributes to personal well-being
- opens up new potential for growth
- develops relationships
- redeems and recreates
- takes us beyond the realm of the functional
- protects us from exalting our work

DEUTERONOMY 5:12–15

Observe the Sabbath day by keeping it holy, as the LORD your God has commanded you. Six days you shall labor and do all your work, but the seventh day is a Sabbath to the LORD your God. On it you shall not do any work, neither you, nor your son or daughter, nor your manservant or maidservant, nor your ox, your donkey or any of your animals, nor the alien within your gates, so that your manservant and maidservant may rest, as you do. Remember that you were slaves in Egypt and that the LORD your God brought you out of there with a mighty hand and an outstretched arm. Therefore the LORD your God has commanded you to observe the Sabbath day.

Questions

1. Why did the Lord make a day of rest?

2. Why did the land need a sabbath rest?

27. Keeping the Sabbath was (and is) a persistent problem.

ISAIAH 58:13–14

If you keep your feet from breaking the Sabbath and from doing as you please on my holy day, if you call the Sabbath a delight and the LORD'S holy day honorable, and if you honor it by not going your own way and not doing as you please or speaking idle words, then you will find your joy in the LORD, and I will cause you to ride on the heights of the land and to feast on the inheritance of your father Jacob.

There is a difference between amusement and recreation. The root meaning of the term "amuse" is "no-think," whereas recreation implies rebuilding and putting things back together.

Questions

1. How have we tended to deal with this issue?

28. The New Testament sets new standards for the use of the Sabbath.

LUKE 6:1–11

One Sabbath Jesus was going through the grainfields, and his disciples began to pick some heads of grain, rub them in their hands and eat the kernels. Some of the Pharisees asked, "Why are you doing what is unlawful on the Sabbath?" Jesus answered them, "Have you never read what David did when he and his companions were hungry? He entered the house of God, and taking the consecrated bread, he ate what is lawful only for priests to eat. And he also gave some to his companions." Then Jesus said to them, "The Son of Man is Lord of the Sabbath."

On another Sabbath he went into the synagogue and was teaching, and a man was there whose right hand was shriveled. The Pharisees and the teachers of the law were looking for a reason to accuse Jesus, so they watched him closely to see if he would heal on the Sabbath. But Jesus knew what they were thinking and said to the man with the shriveled hand, "Get up and stand in front of everyone." So he got up and stood there.

Then Jesus said to them, "I ask you, which is lawful on the Sabbath: to do good or to do evil, to save life or to destroy it?"

He looked around at them all, and then said to the man, "Stretch out your hand." He did so, and his hand was completely restored. But they were furious and began to discuss with one another what they might do to Jesus.

It is very hard not to be busy. Being busy has become a status symbol. People expect us to be busy and to have many things on our minds... being busy and being important often seem to mean the same thing.... In our production-oriented society, being busy... has become one of the main ways, if not the main way, of identifying ourselves.... More enslaving than our occupations, however, are our preoccupations.

Henri Nouwen

LUKE 14:1–5

One Sabbath, when Jesus went to eat in the house of a prominent Pharisee, he was being carefully watched. There in front of him was a man suffering from dropsy. Jesus asked the Pharisees and experts in the law, "Is it lawful to heal on the Sabbath or not?" But they remained silent. So taking hold of the man, he healed him and sent him away.

Then he asked them, "If one of you has a son or an ox that falls into a well on the Sabbath day, will you not immediately pull him out?"

Questions

1. How did Jesus modify and transcend the ways in which the Jews kept the Sabbath?
2. Did he abolish the Sabbath? Why or why not?
3. What is the interplay between rest and work in the light of the concept of the Sabbath?

29 Paul draws attention to different religious interpretations of how we handle the days of the week.

ROMANS 14:5–8

One man considers one day more sacred than another; another man considers every day alike. Each one should be fully convinced in his own mind. He who regards one day as special, does so to the Lord. He who eats meat, eats to the Lord, for he gives thanks to God; and he who abstains, does so to the Lord and gives thanks to God. For none of us lives to himself alone and none of us dies to himself alone. If we live, we live to the Lord; and if we die, we die to the Lord. So, whether we live or die, we belong to the Lord.

> There is time for everything that is in God's plan for each of us. He does not arbitrarily hold us accountable for what he refuses to allow time or space for. As Psalm 138:8 declares, "The Lord will fulfill his purpose for me." This is liberating.

COLOSSIANS 2:16–19

Therefore do not let anyone judge you by what you eat or drink, or with regard to a religious festival, a New Moon celebration or a Sabbath day. These are a shadow of the things that were to come; the reality, however, is found in Christ. Do not let anyone who delights in false humility and the worship of angels disqualify you for the prize. Such a person goes into great detail about what he has seen, and his unspiritual mind puffs him up with idle notions. He has lost connection with the Head, from whom the whole body, supported and held together by its ligaments and sinews, grows as God causes it to grow.

> Most middle-class Americans tend to worship their work, to work at their play, and to play at their worship. As a result, their meanings and values are distorted, their relationships disintegrate faster than they can keep them in repair, and their lifestyles resemble a cast of characters in search of a plot.
>
> *Gordon Dahl*

Questions

1. Considering Paul's teaching, what should be your approach to a day of rest?

2. How do you feel about your activities in relation to this concept of rest? Is it best thought of as a day or as a principle?

30 The cycle of work and rest is part of God's design. There should be a natural rhythm to our lives.

ECCLESIASTES 3:1–8

There is a time for everything, and a season for every activity under heaven: a time to be born and a time to die, a time to plant and a time to uproot, a time to kill and a time to heal, a time to tear down and a time to build, a time to weep and a time to laugh, a time to mourn and a time to dance, a time to scatter stones and a time to gather them, a time to embrace and a time to refrain, a time to search and a time to give up, a time to keep and a time to throw away, a time to tear and a time to mend, a time to be silent and a time to speak, a time to love and a time to hate, a time for war and a time for peace.

> The biblical picture can be contrasted with the industrialized world's drive to escape from work. We manufacture distractions and entertainments, we live for Friday and Saturday nights, we count days to vacations. These activities try to negate work and, hence, are controlled by it. Our most characteristic leisure activity is consumption. . . . Its manufactured 'holidays' (including 'Labor Day') are becoming mere excuses for novel forms of consumption.
>
> *Paul Marshall*

MATTHEW 11:28–30 (THE MESSAGE)

Are you tired? Worn out? Burned out on religion? Come to Me. Get away with Me and you'll recover your life. I'll show you how to take a real rest. Walk with Me and work with Me—watch how I do it. Learn the unforced rhythms of grace. I won't lay anything heavy or ill-fitting on you. Keep company with Me and you'll learn to live freely and lightly.

MATTHEW 11:28–30

Come to me, all you who are weary and burdened, and I will give you rest. Take my yoke upon you and learn from me, for I am gentle and humble in heart, and you will find rest for your souls. For my yoke is easy and my burden is light.

Our politics, religion, news, athletics, education, and commerce have been transformed into congenial adjuncts of show business, largely without protest or even much popular notice. The result is that we are a people on the verge of amusing ourselves to death.

Neil Postman

Questions

1. How do these statements expand and deepen our understanding of the mandate to refresh ourselves?

2. Write down a definition of rest that accords with what you have seen in the Scriptures.

3. How does this compare with the concept of "time off"?

31 When Jesus speaks about rest, it is both physical and spiritual. Rest implies placing our restless turbulence in his hands. Consider the following passages:

PSALM 37:5
Commit your way to the LORD; trust in him and he will do this. . . .

PROVERBS 3:5–6
Trust in the LORD with all your heart and lean not on your own understanding; in all your ways acknowledge him, and he will make your paths straight.

JEREMIAH 6:16
. . . [A]sk where the good way is, and walk in it, and you will find rest for your souls.

The workaholic temperament is characterized by an obsession with work-related activities at the expense of spiritual, social, family and physical priorities. Workaholics may be highly valued in some work cultures.... However, workaholism is in fact a species of immaturity and self-indulgence.

Rodney Green

JOHN 15:1–7

I am the true vine, and my Father is the gardener. He cuts off every branch in me that bears no fruit, while every branch that does bear fruit he prunes so that it will be even more fruitful. You are already clean because of the word I have spoken to you. Remain in me, and I will remain in you. No branch can bear fruit by itself; it must remain in the vine. Neither can you bear fruit unless you remain in me. I am the vine; you are the branches. If a man remains in me and I in him, he will bear much fruit; apart from me you can do nothing. If anyone does not remain in me, he is like a branch that is thrown away and withers; such branches are picked up, thrown into the fire and burned. If you remain in me and my words remain in you, ask whatever you wish, and it will be given you.

Questions

1. What advice would you give to a compulsive workaholic?

2. Why do you think that our culture is so fixated on work? And why do we reward the workaholic?

Why are we so stressed? Perhaps because we are often not "gentle and humble in heart" (Matthew 11:29). We push for ungodly things. We are proud and aggressive. We are self-centered, which destroys our ability to worship God. Yet Jesus raises the question: "What good is it for a man to gain the whole world, yet forfeit his soul?" (Mark 8:36).

But anyone who enters God's rest also rests from his own work (Hebrews 4:10). God's rest is the salvation that he offers.

Disobedience and rebellion shut people out from his kingdom. Today those who are not "humble in heart" are equally disobedient and equally cut off from true rest.

32 Even at the end of time, the biblical concept of rest is foundational.

REVELATION 14:11–13

And the smoke of their torment rises for ever and ever. There is no rest day or night for those who worship the beast and his image, or for anyone who receives the mark of his name." This calls for patient endurance on the part of the saints who obey God's commandments and remain faithful to Jesus.

Then I heard a voice from heaven say, "Write: Blessed are the dead who die in the Lord from now on."

"Yes," says the Spirit, "they will rest from their labor, for their deeds will follow them."

Questions

1. How are heaven and hell contrasted in the scripture above?

33 Numerous authors have addressed the nature of rest and leisure. What can you learn from these writers?

Consider these abbreviated definitions from Webster's Dictionary:

- Rest: Ceasing from work; peace; ease or refreshment; relief or freedom from disturbance; mental or emotional serenity
- Recreation: Refreshment of mind or body after work, re-creation
- Renewal: Making new, restoring, replenishing
- Leisure: Freedom from duties, responsibilities or activities
- Amusement: Entertainment, light or pleasurable diversion

Paul Marshall on the topic of rest:

"Resting is tied to faith—which is one reason why most of us avoid rest.... The Scriptures frequently relate a lack of rest to unbelief (Psalm 95:8–11; Hebrews 3:7–4:10). When we rest, we acknowledge that all our striving will, of itself, do nothing. It means letting the world pass us by for a time. Genuine rest requires acknowledgment that God, and our brothers and sisters, can survive without us. It requires a recognition of our own insufficiency and a handing over of responsibility. It is a real surrender to the ways of God. It is a moment of celebration when we acknowledge that blessing comes only from the hand of God. This is why rest requires faith. It is also why salvation can be pictured as rest...."

Paul Stevens on the topic of leisure:

"At its simplest level, leisure is a diversion providing the opportunity to set aside our normal employment so that we can break out of our routines and experience a needed release.

At a deeper level, leisure provides relaxation and rest, refreshing us for all of life. Slothful people, as well as workaholics, are bored or boring.

Still deeper, leisure is restorative, providing opportunity for creative thoughts, cultivating memories, and gaining perspective. But at its deepest level, leisure is transformative, contributing to our continual conversion into childlike people who enjoy God and delight in God's creation. To understand and experience leisure fully, and to resist trivializing it or turning it into a purely consumer activity as much of popular culture tempts us to do, we must think biblically."

The Oxford Declaration on Christian Faith and Economics *(1990)* says this about how we should cultivate our leisure time:

- Relating to creation: in the enjoyment of nature as God's creation
- Relating to ourselves: in the free exercise and development of our God-given abilities
- Relating to other people: in the cultivation of friendship
- Relating to God: in delighting ourselves in communion with God

Questions

1. How do these observations add to our concept of rest?
2. What are the marks of a good leisure life?
3. Why is it so hard to enter into physical and spiritual rest?
4. When we relax, why do we often feel guilty?
5. At the end of his life, Paul affirmed, "I have fought the good fight, I have finished the race, I have kept the faith" (2 Timothy 4:7). How do we know when our work is finished?
6. How do you plan and use your vacations?

34 There appears to be a principle that still underlies the concept of a sabbath rest.

MATTHEW 11:29–30

Take my yoke upon you and learn from me, for I am gentle and humble in heart, and you will find rest for your souls. For my yoke is easy and my burden is light.

> We are apt to associate the word "school" with "work"... but the word itself means exactly the opposite. It comes from a Greek word *skole*, which means leisure or free-time. A school was understood to be a place... where one was introduced to those activities of explanation and imagination that were 'free' because they were pursued for their own sake and were emancipated from the limitations and anxieties of work.
>
> *Michael Oakeshott*

HEBREWS 4:1–11

Therefore, since the promise of entering his rest still stands, let us be careful that none of you be found to have fallen short of it. For we also have had the gospel preached to us, just as they did; but the message they heard was of no value to them, because those who heard did not combine it with faith. Now we who have believed enter that rest, just as God has said,

"So I declared on oath in my anger, 'They shall never enter my rest.'"

And yet his work has been finished since the creation of the world. For somewhere he has spoken about the seventh day in these words: "And on the seventh day God rested from all his work." And again in the passage above he says, "They shall never enter my rest."

It still remains that some will enter that rest, and those who formerly had the gospel preached to them did not go in, because of their disobedience. Therefore God again set a certain day, calling it Today, when a long time later he spoke through David, as was said before:

"Today, if you hear his voice, do not harden your hearts."

For if Joshua had given them rest, God would not have spoken later about another day. There remains, then, a Sabbath-rest for the people of God; for anyone who enters God's rest also rests from his own work, just as God did from his. Let us, therefore, make every effort to enter that rest, so that no one will fall by following their example of disobedience.

Questions

1. What is this principle and does it still prevail?

35 True rest is the negation of worry. How does Jesus address this?

MATTHEW 6:25–34

Therefore I tell you, do not worry about your life, what you will eat or drink; or about your body, what you will wear. Is not life more important than food, and the body more important than clothes? Look at the birds of the air; they do not sow or reap or store away in barns, and yet your heavenly Father feeds them. Are you not much more valuable than they? Who of you by worrying can add a single hour to his life?

And why do you worry about clothes? See how the lilies of the field grow. They do not labor or spin. Yet I tell you that not even Solomon in all his splendor was dressed like one of these. If that is how God clothes the grass of the field, which is here today and tomorrow is thrown into the fire, will he not much more clothe you, O you of little faith? So do not worry, saying, 'What shall we eat?' or 'What shall we drink?' or 'What shall we wear?' For the pagans run after all these things, and your heavenly Father knows that you need them.

But seek first his kingdom and his righteousness, and all these things will be given to you as well. Therefore do not worry about tomorrow, for tomorrow will worry about itself. Each day has enough trouble of its own.

Jesus does not respond to our worry-filled way of living by saying that we should not be so busy with worldly affairs. He does not try to pull us away from the many events, activities, and people that make up our lives.

He does not tell us that what we do is unimportant, valueless, or useless. Nor does he suggest that we should withdraw from our involvements and live quiet, restful lives removed from the struggles of the world. . . . Jesus' response to our worry-filled lives is quite different. He asks us to shift the point of gravity, to relocate the center of our attention, to change our priorities. Jesus wants us to move from the 'many things' to the 'one necessary thing.' Jesus does not speak about a change of activities, a change in contacts, or even a change of pace. He speaks about a change of heart. . . . What counts is where our hearts are. When we worry, we have our hearts in the wrong place. Jesus asks us to move our hearts to the center, where all other things fall into place.

What is this center? Jesus calls it the kingdom, the kingdom of his Father.

Henri Nouwen

MATTHEW 13:22

The one who received the seed that fell among the thorns is the man who hears the word, but the worries of this life and the deceitfulness of wealth choke it, making it unfruitful.

LUKE 10:38–42

As Jesus and his disciples were on their way, he came to a village where a woman named Martha opened her home to him. She had a sister called

Mary, who sat at the Lord's feet listening to what he said. But Martha was distracted by all the preparations that had to be made. She came to him and asked, "Lord, don't you care that my sister has left me to do the work by myself? Tell her to help me!"

"Martha, Martha," the Lord answered, "you are worried and upset about many things, but only one thing is needed. Mary has chosen what is better, and it will not be taken away from her."

JAMES 4:13–15

Now listen, you who say, "Today or tomorrow we will go to this or that city, spend a year there, carry on business and make money." Why, you do not even know what will happen tomorrow. What is your life? You are a mist that appears for a little while and then vanishes. Instead, you ought to say, "If it is the Lord's will, we will live and do this or that."

Questions

1. What is the essence of Jesus' advice on how to deal with worry?

2. What is a healthy attitude when under pressure or uncertainty?

36 Jesus understood the need that his colleagues had for rest.

MARK 6:30–32

. . . because so many people were coming and going that they did not even have a chance to eat, he said to them, "Come with me by yourselves to a quiet place and get some rest." So they went away by themselves in a boat to a solitary place.

Questions

1. Notice the elements in this account that can guide us into satisfying rest: Come with me . . . by yourselves . . . to a quiet place . . . and get some rest. . . . Which element seems hardest for you? How can you arrange your affairs to secure such rest?

37 True rest occurs when we entrust ourselves to God, when we abide in Jesus Christ. What is the interplay of grace and obedience in finding this rest?

ISAIAH 55:1-3

Come, all you who are thirsty, come to the waters; and you who have no money, come, buy and eat! Come, buy wine and milk without money and without cost. Why spend money on what is not bread, and your labor on what does not satisfy? Listen, listen to me, and eat what is good, and your soul will delight in the richest of fare. Give ear and come to me; hear men, that your soul may live.

MATTHEW 11:28–30

Come to me, all you who are weary and burdened, and I will give you rest. Take my yoke upon you and learn from me, for I am gentle and humble in heart, and you will find rest for your souls. For my yoke is easy and my burden is light.

One of the most notable characteristics of worrying is that it fragments our lives. . . . Jesus responds to this condition of being filled yet unfulfilled, very busy yet unconnected, all over the place yet never at home. He wants to bring us to the place where we belong. But his call to live a spiritual life can only be heard when we are willing honestly to confess our own homeless and worrying existence and recognize its fragmenting effect on our daily life. Only then can a desire for our true home develop. It is of this desire that Jesus speaks when he says, 'Do not worry . . . set your hearts on his kingdom first…and all these other things will be given you as well.'

Henri Nouwen

JOHN 15:4–8

Remain in me, and I will remain in you. No branch can bear fruit by itself; it must remain in the vine. Neither can you bear fruit unless you remain in me. I am the vine; you are the branches. If a man remains in me and I in him, he will bear much fruit; apart from me you can do nothing. If anyone does not remain in me, he is like a branch that is thrown away and withers; such branches are picked up, thrown into the fire and burned. If you remain in me and my words remain in you, ask whatever you wish, and it will be given you. This is to my Father's glory, that you bear much fruit, showing yourselves to be my disciples.

TITUS 3:5-8

. . . he saved us, not because of righteous things we had done, but because of his mercy. He saved us through the washing of rebirth and renewal by the Holy Spirit, whom he poured out on us generously through Jesus Christ our Savior, so that, having been justified by his grace, we might become heirs having the hope of eternal life. This is a trustworthy saying. And I want you to stress these things, so that those who have trusted in God may be careful to devote themselves to doing what is good. These things are excellent and profitable for everyone.

GALATIANS 5:22-25

But the fruit of the Spirit is love, joy, peace, patience, kindness, goodness, faithfulness, gentleness and self-control. Against such things there is no law. Those who belong to Christ Jesus have crucified the sinful nature, its passions and desires. Since we live by the Spirit, let us keep in step with the Spirit. Let us not become conceited, provoking and envying each other.

ROMANS 5:1-2

Therefore, since we have been justified through faith, we have peace with God through our Lord Jesus Christ, through whom we have gained access by faith into this grace in which we now stand...

Questions

1. What practical guidance does Jesus give us for abiding in him?

2. How have these principles in this section enhanced your commitment to biblical rest?

Yale professor Miroslav Volf pointed to a subtle force in modern culture that deprives us of true inner rest. He said: "Work thrives today more on the insatiable hunger for self-realization than on the Protestant work ethic. In their own eyes and in the eyes of their contemporaries, modern human beings are what they do. The kind of work they do and what they accomplish or acquire through work provide a basic key to their identity."

In other words, our culture operates on a "you are what you do" mentality. If we view work as the basis for generating our self-worth and identity, then what happens to us when we can no longer work, or if we are unemployed? What if our work is deemed by society to be "menial"?

We see this struggle in the following case studies of two workers in similar lines of work. Both stories were published in the classic book on work titled *Working*, by Studs Terkel, in 1974.

A.

"People ask me what I do. I say, 'I drive a garbage truck for the city.' They call you G-man or, 'How's business picking up?' Just the standard. I have nothing to be ashamed of. I put in my eight hours. We make a pretty good salary. I feel I earn my money. I can go any place I want. I conduct myself as a gentleman any place I go. My wife is happy, this is the big thing. She doesn't look down at me."

Nick Salerno

B.

"Right now I'm doing work that I detest. I'm a janitor. It's a dirty job. You work hard. This is the kind of work I used to think hillbillies or DPs would do. You don't associate with people like that. Now I'm one of them. 'You're a bum'—this is the picture I have of myself. I'm a flop because of what I've come to. . . . It's a dead end. . . . I feel inferior."

Tim Devlin

38 Meditate on the following passage and observe how God's grace inverts the world's perspective on work and human value.

EPHESIANS 2:8-10

For it is by grace you have been saved, through faith—and this not from yourselves, it is the gift of God—not by works, so that no one can boast. For we are God's workmanship, created in Christ Jesus to do good works, which God prepared in advance for us to do.

No Christian should despise his position and life if he is living in accordance with the Word of God.

Martin Luther

Questions

1. What role does work play in your sense of self-worth and identity?

2. To save us by grace, it cost God the life of his Son. In this sacrfice, God declares our immeasurable value independent of our work. What does God's declaration of our value free us from having to do? What does this freedom mean in terms of inner rest?

3. The scripture above says that we are "created in Christ Jesus to do good works." Now that our value and identity have been established securely in Christ, what should be our ultimate motivation for work?

"The spirituality of work is a disciplined attempt to align ourselves and our environment with God and to incarnate God's spirit in the world through all the effort, 'paid and unpaid,' we exert to make the world a better place, a little closer to the way God would have things."

Gregory Pierce

"We want to be one of the three leading companies in women's fashion wear in Slovakia. In our work we want to respect biblical values. We see our work as an opportunity to serve the people of our nation by our products, but also by the high quality of sales and services, as well as by the message. Jesus said to go into all the world to make disciples. Our world is the garment industry."

Renata & Miro Kuban

"May the favor of the Lord our God rest upon us; establish the work of our hands for us—yes, establish the work of our hands."

Psalm 90:17

Section Notes

Taking Action

A true adventure with God, one in which we participate in God's purposes, requires us to put his counsel and designs into practice in every arena. We are called to integrate our professions with God's purposes. God wants us to live, not just learn. We need to begin taking tangible steps toward applying—at work and at home—what he is teaching us.

This is rarely accomplished alone. If you have studied this book with a group of friends, you have an opportunity to think together about how to apply the truths you've discovered so far. A suggestion is to choose one or two principles from this study that most impacted you. Then talk as a group about how you might live out those principles in the context of your work, family, and community. Hopefully, this group of friends can be an ongoing source of encouragement and growth for one another.

The following questions might help guide you in this process.

1. Review this study, including your personal notes, and identify several principles or truths that most impacted your mind and heart. What are these principles and why are they important to you?

2. Looking at your situation and context, what needs to take place in order for you to begin to live differently? What obstacles and risks do you encounter as you contemplate making changes in your work and family?

3. Thinking beyond your personal needs, what can you do to improve the lives of those around you? What needs do you see in your profession and workplace? Think about how to apply these principles in your work and within your broader sphere of influence. Be creative and innovative.

4. Participate with your friends to seek an adventure with God together. What are you learning together from your experiences? The writer of Hebrews wrote: "And let us consider how we may spur one another on toward love and good deeds, not giving up meeting together . . . ." Be committed to one another for the long-term, encouraging each other to innovate ways of doing good through your work and professions.

Bibliography of Works Cited

Applebaum, Herbert. *The Concept of Work,* (State University of New York Press, 1992).

Arendt, Hannah. *The Human Condition,* (University of Chicago, 1958).

Banks, Robert. *God the Worker: Journeys into the Mind, Heart and Imagination of God,* (Judson Press, 1994).

Bergel, Gary. *Crosswinds,* issue of summer 1995.

Blamires, Harry. *The Christian Mind,* (Servant Books, 1978).

Browning, Elizabeth Barrett. *Aurora Leigh,* J. Miller, 1864.

Carlyle, Thomas. *Past and Present,* 1843.

Chewning, Richard, editor. *Biblical Principles & Business: The Practice, Vol. 3,* NavPress 1990…source of quotation from Packer.

Clancy, William. Review in *Commonwealth of Leisure, The Basis of Culture,* 1952.

Coolidge, Calvin. Quoted in *Thoughts on Prosperity* in *The Forbes Leadership Library,* (Triumph Books, 1996).

Dahl, Gordon. *Work, Play, and Worship in a Leisure-Oriented Society,* (Augsburg, 1972), p. 12.

Danker, William. *Profit for the Lord,* (Eerdmans, 1971), quotation from Wesley.

de Grazia, Sebastian. *Of Time, Work and Leisure,* (Anchor Books, 1962).

Devlin, Tim. Quoted in *Working,* by Studs Terkel, (Pantheon Books, 1974).

DePree, Max. *Leadership Jazz,* (Doubleday, 1992).

DeThomasis, Louis & William Ammentorp. *Paradigms and Parables: The Ten Commandments for Ethics in Business,* (HRD Press, 1995).

Donkin, Richard. *Blood, Sweat and Tears: The Evolution of Work,* (Texere, 2001), p. 323.

Dumbrell, William. "Creation, Covenant and Work" in *Crux* 24, September, 1988.

Dwight, John Sullivan. *Working,* quoted in *Bartlett's Familiar Quotations, 14th Edition,* (Little, Brown and Company, 1968), p. 675.

Ellul, Jacques. *The Presence of the Kingdom,* (Helmers & Howard, 1989), p. 7.

Ellul, Jacques. *To Will and To Do,* (Pilgrim Press, 1969), p. 107–108.

Glanz, Barbara. "Developing Your Personal Signature" in *Heart at Work,* by Jack Canfield & Jacqueline Miller, (McGraw Hill, 1996), p. 8.

Green, Rodney. *90,000 Hours: Managing the World of Work,* (Scripture Union, 2002), p. 55.

Guinness, Os. *The Call,* (Word, 1998), p. 46.

Hardy, Lee. *The Fabric of This World,* (Eerdmans, 1990).

Heschel, Abraham. "The Sabbath," quoted in *Working,* edited by Gilbert Meilaender, (Notre Dame Press, 2000), p. 261, 263.

Houston, James. *The Transforming Power of Prayer,* (NavPress, 1996).

Kidner, Derek. *Genesis: An Introduction & Commentary,* (Tyndale, 1967), p. 78.

Kusnierik, Jurai. *Integrity in Business in Post-Communist Central Europe,* 1995.

Lewis, C.S. *The Weight of Glory,* (Eerdmans, 1949).

Lewis, C.S. *Letters to an American Lady,* (Eerdmans, 1967).

Lewis, C.S. *The World's Last Night,* (Harcourt Brace, 1960).

Livingstone, David. "Cambridge Lectures," (Deighton, Bell & Co., 1860).

Luther, Martin. Quoted in *Embodied Holiness: The Spirituality of Daily Life,* by Paul Stevens.

MacLeod, George. *Only One Way Left,* (Iona Community, 1956), p. 38.

Marshall, Paul. "Calling, Work and Rest," *Christian Faith and Practice in the Modern World,* (Eerdmans, 1988).

Marshall, Paul & Others. *Labour of Love: Essays on Work,* (Wedge Foundation, 1980).

Middelmann, Udo. *Proexistence,* (InterVarsity Press, 1974).

Minear, Paul. *Images of the Church in the New Testament,* (Westminster Press, 1960).

Moore, R. Laurence. *Selling God,* (Oxford, 1994).

Nash, Laura. *Believers in Business,* (Thomas Nelson, 1994).

Novak, Michael. *Business as a Calling,* (Free Press, 1996).

Nouwen, Henri J.M. *Making All Things New,* (Harper Collins, 1981).

Oakeshott, Michael. "Work and Play," in *First Things*, Institute on Religion and Public Life.

Oxford Declaration on Christian Faith and Economics, 1990.

Osler, William. Quoted in *Life of Sir William Osler*, by Harvey Cushing.

Packer, J.I. *Knowing and Doing the Will of God*, (Servant, 1995).

Penzias, Arno. Quoted in Cosmos, Bios, and Theos, Henry Margenau and Roy Varghese, editors, (Open Court, 1992), p. 83.

Peterson, Eugene. *The Message, New Testament with Psalms*, (NavPress, 1994).

Peterson, Eugene. *Living the Resurrection*, (NavPress, 2006), p. 31-33.

Phillips, Rick. "Jessie's Glove" in *Heart at Work*, by Jack Canfield & Jacqueline Miller, (McGraw Hill, 1996).

Pieper, Josef. *Leisure: The Basis of Culture*, (St. Augustine's Press, 1998), p. 33.

Pierce, Gregory. *Spirituality @ Work*, (Loyola Press, 2001), p. 19.

Pope John Paul II. *Laborem Exercens, Encyclical On Human Work*, (U.S. Conference of Catholic Bishops, 1981).

Postman, Neil. *Amusing Ourselves to Death*, (Penguin, 1986), p. 4.

Preece, Gordon. Article on work in *The Complete Book of Everyday Christianity*, (InterVarsity Press, 1997).

Russ, Daniel. Introduction to *The Machine Stops*, by E.M. Forster, (Trinity Forum, 2000), p. 5.

Ryken, Leland. *Work and Leisure in Christian Perspective*, (Multnomah, 1987).

St. Patrick's Breastplate. Quoted in *Crux*, (Regent College, Dec. 1996), p 28.

Salerno, Nick. Quoted in *Working*, by Studs Terkel, (Pantheon Books, 1974).

Sayers, Dorothy L. "Why Work?" in *Creed or Chaos?*, (Sophia Inst., 1999), p. 67, 89, 101, 105, 106, 108.

Sayers, Dorothy L. *Essays Presented to Charles Williams*, (Ayer Company, 1947).

Sayers, Dorothy L. "Vocation in Work" in *A Christian Basis for the Post-war World*, (SCM Press, 1942).

Schroeder, Gerald. *The Science of God: The Convergence of Scientific and Biblical Wisdom*, (Broadway Books, 1998), p. 102, 124.

Second Vatican Council. *Pastoral Constitution on the Church in the Modern*

World (Gaudium et Spes), section 35, by Pope Paul VI (Pauline Books & Media, 1965), page 33.

Sherman, Doug and Hendricks, William. *Your Work Matters to God,* (NavPress, 1987).

Stevens, R. Paul. "Articles on Leisure and Sabbath" in *The Complete Book of Everyday Christianity,* (InterVarsity Press, 1997).

Stevens, R. Paul. *The Equipper's Guide to Every-Member Ministry,* (InterVarsity Press, 1992).

Stevens, R. Paul. "Theology of Work: Curse, Blessing or Idol," Undated Essay.

Stevens, R. Paul. *The Other Six Days,* (Eerdmans, 2000), p. 248.

Stott, John. "Work and Unemployment," Sermon; 18 Feb. 1979.

Stott, John. *The Message of Romans,* (InterVarsity Press, 1994).

Stott, John. *Issues Facing Christians Today,* (Marshall Pickering, 1990).

Tilgher, Adriano. *Work: What it Has Meant to Men Through the Ages,* (Harrap and Co., 1931), p. 39.

Volf, Miroslav. *Work in the Spirit: Towards a Theology of Work,* (Oxford, 1991).

Weber, Max. *The Protestant Ethic and the Spirit of Capitalism,* (Allen & Unwin, 1930).

Westhead, Nigel. "Evangelicals and Sabbath Keeping in the 1990s," in *Evangel,* (Paternoster Periodicals), Summer 1995.

White, Jerry & Mary. *On the Job: Survival or Satisfaction,* (NavPress, 1988).

Whitman, Walt. *Song of Myself,* published in *The American Tradition in Literature, 6th Edition,* edited by George Perking, et al., (Random House, 1985), p. 27-63.

www.ingramcontent.com/pod-product-compliance
Lightning Source LLC
Chambersburg PA
CBHW020909080526
44589CB00011B/509